The Autobiography of Sant Bahinabai

THE AUTOBIOGRAPHY OF SANT BAHINABAI

Translated & Introduced by

Chandrakant Kaluram Mhatre

Sitaram Mhatre Foundation

Navi Mumbai

The Autobiography of Sant Bahinabai

Translated & Introduced by
Chandrakant Kaluram Mhatre

Published by
SITARAM MHATRE FOUNDATION
Registered Office
Sitaram Smaran, 896, Sector 19B,
Koparkhairane, Navi Mumbai 400709
Email: info@sitarammhatre.foundation

First Edition January 2023
ISBN   (Paperback) 978-81-960911-1-8
ISBN   (eBook) 978-81-960911-0-1

Printed at
Createspace

Cover, Typesetting & Book Design
Chandrakant Kaluram Mhatre

To my baby sisters,
Chandrakala, Aruna & Grishma

CONTENTS

INTRODUCTION

Thanks to its Varkari heritage, Maharashtra has a very long tradition of women poets, beginning with the likes of Muktabai and Janabai as early as in the final decades of the thirteenth century. When the rest of the world was busy keeping its womenfolk far, far away from the literary world, poets after poets in Maharashtra were joining this pantheon of women poets to ensure that this unique cultural phenomenon does not get brushed aside as an aberration by the powers that be. Thus, we have Soyarabai, Nirmala, Kanhopatra, too, expressing themselves in what can be termed as the lyrics of the highest order. Not only did they get an opportunity to express themselves but their compositions were also written down and preserved for the centuries to come - no matter how subversive these expressions were. Janabai's abhang throwing open challenge to the patriarchy were as revered in this land as Soyarabai's abhang documenting the brutalities of caste discrimination. No wonder then that this glorious tradition of Varkari women poets culminated in the multifaceted Bahinabai (or Baheni as she calls herself) of the seventeenth century.

How multifaceted was Sant[1] Bahinabai (संत बहिणाबाई)? Here is a glimpse: Bahinabai was born on 25 September 1628 and she breathed her last at noon on 27 September 1700. How can I be so sure about these dates? Bahinabai herself has documented these details in her autobiography. Of course, she is not the first Indian autobiographer; that laurel resides with Sant Namdev who predates her by more than 300 years. However, she is definitely the first Indian woman to write an autobiography. A simple Google search and you will come back at me with Rassundari Devi's *Amar Jiban*. You can do better than that if you dig deeper. What did you find? *Amar Jiban* was published in 1876. Now consider the literary fact that Bahinabai completed her autobiography on 27 September 1700 and it had been in circulation for a whopping 176 years before *Amar Jiban* saw daylight! It is settled then that Sant Bahinabai is the first woman autobiographer of India. That may not be sufficient to call someone multifaceted though, so consider this: Bahinabai translated *Vajrasuchi Upanishad* from Sanskrit into Marathi and it has been in circulation for the last three hundred years, which makes her one of the very first women translators in the entire world. Needless to mention, Sant Bahinabai is the first woman translator of India. Now, if I have piqued your curiosity enough, let's get all serious and try to understand and appreciate the immense contribution this woman poet has made to enrich our world.

Who was Sant Bahinabai?
Sant Bahinabai should not be mistaken with the 20th century Marathi poet Bahinabai Chaudhari. Sant Bahinabai or Bahinabai Pathak (aka Bahinabai Siurkar) was born in a brahmin family of Devgaon village in the Aurangabad District of Maharashtra. Her father was Aauji Kulkarni (आऊजी कुळकर्णी) and her mother's name was Janaki (जानकी). Shockingly, even by the abysmal standards of the seventeenth century, Bahinabai's parents married her off to a thirty-year-old widower when she was just a toddler. Here starts a long series of hardships that Bahinabai had to brave out for the better part of her life. Hardly had she turned seven, when she had to leave their native place along with her

family and go in search of livelihood from village to village and town to town, and that too on foot. No one knew when or where the next meal would be. To worsen the matters, Bahinabai's bad-tempered husband (a male chauvinist proper) accompanied her family during these seemingly endless journeys and Bahinabai was subjected to the most brutal form of domestic violence at the hands of her husband from a very tender age. This travesty of a married life continued for almost a decade and having born in the so-called higher caste did next to nothing to alleviate Bahinabai's misery, just like millions of such women before and after her. What makes Bahinabai's sufferings significant is the fact that she chose to give them a voice in her autobiography:

> Mind was dispirited
> Disliked everything
> But there is no fighting
> With the fate.

Having travelled far and wide from such a young age certainly had shaped Bahinabai's disposition, making her aware of the larger world and the happenings therein. One of these happenings of the time was Tukaram's poems with which she got acquainted as a pre-teen through bhajan-kirtans and was so strongly influenced by them that she craved to meet Tukaram:

> Meeting Tukoba
> Would be the occasion
> Like attaining salvation
> It would be for me.

Once she comes under the influence of Tukaram's poems, her life completely changes and a dreamy teenager transforms into a ferocious rebel challenging the patriarchy and caste-hegemony. She even seems to have won her heroic battle for a little while, only to be crushed by the cowardly tactics of her husband. However, as luck would have it (or by divine intervention, if you like), her surrender proves to be a tactical retreat and her wish is fulfilled at the age of eighteen when she gets to meet Tukaram in person and even receives initiation at his hands:

> Baheni says his hand
> He placed on my head
> The body in this world
> Didn't seem to exist.

I am aware this reads more like a script of an overly dramatic young adult movie but that is exactly how dramatic Bahinabai's life was and it is to her great credit that she does not let her autobiography sound melodramatic even for an instance. Her autobiography does not capitalise on her hardships and her sufferings, rather it celebrates her immense mental strength with which she overcame all of them and attained the goal that she had set out for herself as a little girl all of eleven.

Bahinabai lived a long life of 72 years and attained such an exalted spiritual status that multiple religious sects have laid claim to her legacy, although her own autobiography and other abhang declare allegiance only to Tukaram and his Varkari teachings. Significantly enough, she named her only son as Vitthal, the paramount deity of the Varkaris and, during her final moments, she chose to listen to the recitation of Dnyaneshwari, the paramount text of the Varkaris:

> I wish to listen now
> To entire *Dnyaneshwari*
> For I am left with
> A few moments.

There is no room for doubt that Bahinabai lived her entire life as a devout Varkari and she took leave of this world as a devout Varkari. As there are people today, who latch onto every possible opportunity to describe Sant Dnyandev as a brahmin while conveniently ignoring the historical facts that it was the brahmins who drove Dnyandev and his entire family out of the community and caused them immense hardships, it was the brahmins who forced Dnyandev's innocent parents to commit suicide, and it was the same brahmins who opposed the right to rite of upanayan for Dnyandev and his brothers to such an extent that they never underwent this rite in their entire life; similarly there have been people trying to hijack Bahinabai's legacy, harping upon her brahminical lineage, nonchalantly overlooking the historical fact that this brahminical lineage was challenged in Bahinabai's own lifetime and her entire family was persecuted systematically being labelled as lowly-borne:

> Are you of goldsmiths
> Or *golak* by caste
> You have no privileges
> Of the brahmins.

It is specifically for the people of this ilk that Bahinabai undertook the translation of *Vajrasuchi*, and declared their entire kind to be unfit to be called as a brahmin:

> Baheni says caste
> Never makes the brahmin
> Key to brahminness
> Is very different.

Bahinabai's poems were first published in print by D. V. Umarkhane in 1913 as *The Poems of Santh Bahinabai: A Great Renowned Sage of Shivpur* (although the title of this book is in

English, its contents are pure Marathi). He was the "Head Clerk Post Office, Khamgaon " as declared on the cover page of the book and had obtained the manuscript from Bahinabai's contemporary descendants at Shiur. Interestingly, this cover page also declares the edition to be the "First Part" of a series, but neither the next part ever came out nor there is a mention of what was supposed to be in the next part. After 13 years of this publication, V. N. Kolharkar published his *Sant Bahinabaicha Gatha* in 1926. There is not much information available about him, apart from having authored *Gaincha Akrosh* in 1922, a booklet about conservation of cows. More unfortunately, he did not bother to mention the provenance of the manuscript(s) in his custody. Apart from a few variations that can be attributed to copying errors, both these texts are similar to great extent, but the Kolharkar Text contains some 147 abhang that are not to be found in the Umarkhane Text. After these two gentlemen, it was Shalini Javadekar who published her *Sant Bahenabaincha Gatha* in 1979 along with an expansive introduction. Her efforts were more critical and scholarly than her predecessors, but she has taken great many liberties with Bahinabai's abhang, going to such an extent as breaking up multiple abhang and then reconstructing one that she finds more coherent.[2] Therefore, for my translation, I have mainly relied on the Kolharkar Text, with some critical inputs from the Umarkhane Text.

Why translate Bahinabai? Again??

It was Justin E. Abbott who first translated Bahinabai's abhang into English, published in 1929 as *Bahinabai: A Translation of Her Autobiography & Verses*. Abbot, like J. N. Fraser who translated Tukaram in 1915, happens to be a pioneer in translating Marathi Bhakti literature in the first half of the 20th century. While the class of the Marathi people who had mastered English back then were busy reaping the rich fruits of this newfound language by serving their colonial masters, these two gentlemen - from the USA and England respectively - were doing their best to preserve & propagate the centuries old Bhakti literature heritage of Marathi by the means of translation. Therefore, I have nothing but the highest praise for Abbott's pioneering attempts at translating Bahinabai's abhang.

Having said that, when assessed critically, Abbott's translation lays bare certain shortcomings that need to be addressed here. His rudimentary understanding of the seventeenth century Marathi language is pardonable, since most of the Marathi speakers fail to comprehend that form of their mother tongue. His enthusiastic but bare minimum acquaintance with the Marathi culture in general and Varkari literary tradition in particular is also permissible, after all such a bilingual literary giant as Dilip Chitre has ended up - quite horrendously - putting "crocodile-shaped rings"[3] in Vitthal's ears in his critically acclaimed & trailblazing translation *Says Tuka* (Note for the uninitiated: Vitthal has been wearing only fish-shaped jewels in his ears for no less than 28 yugas). However, what is utterly unforgivable is Abbott's treatment of Bahinabai's abhang as mere "verses". He fails to see Bahinbai's abhang as lyrics, let alone appreciate them as lyrics of the highest order. Result? He ends up paraphrasing her exquisitely poignant poems, rendering nothing but lifeless corpses in his translation.

Moreover, it has been almost a century since last English translation of Bahinabai's poems and that itself speaks volumes about the extent of neglect that Bahinabai has suffered at the hands of her own Marathi speaking people. This translation is a small effort to remedy that unfortunate situation, with the hope that it will rekindle a new interest in Bahinabai's poems, grab attention of young translators and result in newer, better translations in near future.

Bahinabai: The Autobiographer

The most significant feature of Bahinabai's autobiography is her awareness of this literary form. It is apparent that she was well acquainted with Namdev's autobiographical abhang. She had most certainly known Tukaram's autobiographical poems by heart (one keeps hearing echoes of Tukaram's abhang throughout *Bahinabai's Gatha*). From her abhang, it is evident that she sets out on this literary endeavour knowing well what she wants to achieve thereby. In her *Gatha*, her autobiographical abhang are found under the section titled as "Atma-charitra" (आत्म-चरित्र - autobiography) in the Umarkhane Text and "Atmanivedan" (आत्मनिवेदन - confessions) in the Kolharkar Text. Out of these two terms, Atmanivedan is closer to the tone that Bahinabai adopts throughout her abhang, interacting with her listener(s) time and again:

> Devgaon is the place
> Of my parents, dear friend
> To the East of which
> Verul lies.

As you can see, her listener is a close friend who seems to have requested Bahinabai to recount the happenings of her illustrious life. From the extant abhang, it is quite clear that this would have happened at least twice, at two totally different times. The first attempt at a younger age is quite straightforward as exemplified by abhang 2 of this translation, which is found only in the Kolharkar Text. Abhang 1 of this translation seems to be the beginning of Bahinabai's second attempt at autobiography at a much later age, with a more exalted tone and a more elaborate style, a plausible outcome of pursuant perusal of Varkari literature, right from Dnyandev through Ekanath to Tukaram.

These 25 autobiographical abhang from the speculative first attempt are found at the end of Atmanivedan section (comprising 53 abhang) of the Kolharkar Text. Many of them recount the same happenings narrated in the first 53 abhang, e.g. abhang 27 in the Kolharkar Text narrates the same happenings which are already narrated in abhang 17-26. Apparently, this abhang originally formed part of another attempt by Bahinabai at documenting her life. For the sake of the continuity of the narrative, I have included this abhang in Appendix II. For the same reason, I have also rearranged the order of the remaining 77 abhang in my translation.

A third section of Bahinabai's autobiographical abhang is found under the title "Niryanache Abhang" in the Umarkhane Text (35 abhang) and "Niryanpar Abhang" in the Kolharkar Text (37 abhang). The listener for this section is Bahinabai's son Vitthal and perhaps other near and dear ones, add to this the fact that Bahinabai is literally bidding farewell here, so in this section, you get abhang that are totally different in tone and style. It is difficult to not get goosebumps each time I read this section knowing their significance in Bahinabai's life. These abhang are also unique in the world of autobiographies because they were composed in the last five days of Bahinabai's life, making Bahinabai's autobiography strikingly distinct in the sense that it is arguably the only autobiography in the world that ends with the last breaths of its writer. Quite interestingly, Kolharkar seems to have understood the autobiographical significance of this section and has put it right after the Atmanivedan section, whereas

Umarkhane has put this section at the end of his book with Atma-charitra at the very beginning and Javadekar has put 119 abhang between these two autobiographical sections.

Bahinabai: The Translator

Being a brahmin by birth does not seem to have benefited Bahinabai much, but it certainly created a great many obstacles in her spiritual life - the biggest being the vehement opposition of the caste-brahmins to her following Tukaram as her Guru. In the seventeenth century, no one would have ever imagined a young brahmin woman getting so subversive to touch the feet of a non-brahmin and that is exactly what Bahinabai did right in front of everyone's eyes. Of course, she was not the first brahmin to lay prostrate before Tukaram. Renowned brahmins of the time such as Rameshwar Bhat were doing that three times a day, singing his eulogies, way before Bahinabai's arrival in Dehu. However, a young brahmin woman all of 18 years doing the same must have sounded like the final nail in the coffin of their birth privileges for the caste-brahmins. No wonder, caste-supremacists like Mambaji sought every possible opportunity to draw her out of Tukaram's influence or drive her out of the bounds of Dehu by every possible means. Conversely, Bahinabai got the opportunity to see up close the filthiness of the thoughts and actions of the privileged people like Mambaji and compare it with Tukaram's completely opposite teachings and practice thereof. This must have made her question: Who is the real brahmin of these two?

She found her answers in the *Vajrasuchi Upanishad*, a Sanskrit treatise that holds the distinction of being the first anti-discrimination Sanskrit text. On one hand, in this philosophical attack on the birth privileges of the caste-brahmin, Bahinabai found the answer to the objection of the caste brahmin: How can a non-brahmin (or *shudra*[4]) like Tukaram become Guru of the brahmins like Bahinabai?

Baheni says the examination
Of deeds designated reveals
The brahminness lies beyond
Deeds designated.

On the other hand, in *Vajrasuchi Upanishad*'s sublime definition of brahminness, she could clearly recognise Tukaram in his thoughts and actions to be the very personification of that brahminness:

Perceives the Supreme Being
Among all living beings
The very personification who is
Of equanimity

Baheni says just like
The sky is everywhere
The brahmin commingles
With the world.

Before I put forward my assessment of Bahinabai as a translator, I would like to clarify yet another widespread misconception about Bahinabai here. It is believed, quite thoughtlessly, that Bahinabai has translated Ashvaghosha's *Vajrasuchi*[5], a Buddhist text. She has not. Bahinabai has translated the *Vajrasuchi Upanishad*, a Vedanta text. It is needless to say that these are two different texts but even established scholars have ended up ascribing *Vajrasuchi Upanishad* to Ashvaghosha. One does not have to do much to verify this fact, just get hold of Bahinabai's Marathi *Vajrasuchi*, Ashvaghosha's Sanskrit

Vajrasuchi and the Sanskrit *Vajrasuchi Upanishad*, then put them side by side. Even if you are not a skilled translator and even if you do not have in-depth understanding of Sanskrit, you will still be able to perceive the abhang-by-abhang movement of Bahinabai's translation running parallel to paragraph-by-paragraph movement of the prose *Vajrasuchi Upanishad*. And you will be able to see for yourself that Bahinabai's text does not include any of the multitudinous expositions that Ashvaghosha's text adds to the philosophical formulations presented in the *Vajrasuchi Upanishad*. The only similarity between Bahinabai's text and Ashvaghosh's text is that both of these texts attack caste-discrimination, but that is only because both of them draw upon the *Vajrasuchi Upanishad* that attacks caste-discrimination.

Having that settled, let's return to Bahinabai's translation of *Vajrasuchi Upanishad*. Bahinabai's clarity of expresseions, her logical progression of arguments in her translation makes me marvel at her impeccable understanding of her source text. To translate well you need to understand your source text really well, you need to relate with it on as many levels as possible - that is how I perceive the translation process and that seems to be how Bahinabai has approached her translation. Basically, Bahinabai's translation is as loyal to its source as a translation could get in those times and still, it is rendered so effortlessly that unless told specifically, one would not be able to tell it to be a translation of some other text. Here, I cannot stop myself from mentioning Dnyandev's own assessment of his *Dnyaneswari* vis-a-vis Vyasa's Bhagavad Gita, where he declares his Marathi version of the Gita to be as good as Vyasa's Sanskrit *Gita*[6]. Bahinabai does not mention it anywhere, but in my professional opinion, her Marathi version of *Vajrasuchi Upanishad* is as good as Sanskrit *Vajrasuchi Upanishad*! However, it is a bit tricky situation here as I am presenting to you my English translation of Bahinabai's Marathi translation of a Sanskrit text, so if you come across any difficulties/oddities in its flow, please remember that they are entirely the shortcomings of my translation, not Bahinabai's.

Bahinabai: The Great-Grandmother of Feminism

For the sake of perspective, let us remind ourselves here that Mary Wollstonecraft published her *A Vindication of the Rights of Woman: with Strictures on Political and Moral Subjects* in 1792 and demanded the right to commensurate education for the women in England. That makes Bahinabai's autobiography about 100 years older than that prototypical text of modern feminism. Now look at what Bahinabai says about the condition of women in India in the seventeenth century:

> Borne as a human though
> In the form of a woman
> Seems to be culmination
> Of uncountable sins
>
> Deprived of the right
> To studying scriptures
> *Gayatri* is hidden away
> By the brahmins.

Anyone who is remotely familiar with Wollstonecraft's proverbial ground-breaking text will see the uncanny resemblance Bahinabai's these words carry with the central arguments of that text. What I am driving here at is the need for an in-depth study of Bahinabai's autobiography from the feminist perspective, which is replete with gems such as the lines mentioned above.

Since my complete incompetence at feminist criticism is abundantly exposed in the last paragraph, I do not need to pretend anymore to do that and we can go about appreciating Bahinabai as a subversive voice from the seventeenth century. Being born a woman in the so-called higher castes most certainly has its privileges like being relatively shielded from the predatory elements of those echelons, that freely prey upon other not-so-privileged women. However, that also means relatively more restrictions within and without the four walls, along with extra burden of the strictures of the scriptures:

> Tender of age
> Considered puerile
> In the terror of the Vedas
> Rendered silent

and

> All the Vedas call out
> The Puranas clamour
> In the company of a woman
> Nothing to gain

> I am nothing
> But a woman's body
> How do I find now
> The Path Supreme?[7]

The challenge that Janabai threw at the patriarchy in the thirteenth century takes on a much more profound form in

Bahinabai's words when she calls the Vedas and puranas out as the source of her oppression. Her identification of the scriptures as the ideological state apparatus for women's oppression is truly Gramscian and significant, given that the bhakti literature tradition in India goes back to almost five hundred years before Bahinabai and she happens to be the first woman to call a spade a spade in this regard, and that too in no uncertain terms. She does not stop just pointing finger at the scripture but goes on to lay bare the multiple levels on which this oppression takes place for a married woman when her marriage takes the form of shackles around her feet by the very dictates of those scriptures:

> The Vedas proclaim
> Do not abandon duties
> But serving the Lord
> Is what I love.

It would have been a wonder only if extreme measures were not taken to suppress such a rebellious voice in the patriarchal framework of the seventeenth century and in Bahinabai's case those measures turned out to be extremely brutal domestic violence. Here my non-existent scholarship in trauma studies does not need to be exposed, but I have no doubt that Bahinabai's autobiography will rank very high among those works that document the lives of survivors of domestic violence, apart from being one of the oldest, if not the oldest, such an account in the history of world literature:

> To his heart's content
> He beat me rigorously
> Tying my hands and legs
> Threw me aside.

What makes me appreciate this woman's spirit more and more is the fact that even the most brutal beating does not deter her from raising more questions:

> Unstoppable, beating me
> The cow bellowed
> The calf too wailed
> Grief-stricken
>
> This all happened
> When I was eighteen
> Had I fallen short
> Fulfilling my duties?

One can only imagine how Bahinabai would have coped with this kind of inhuman treatment during her pregnancy, and that too with no support even from her parents, since her husband would beat her up right in front of their eyes and they would not even raise as much a finger to stop him. Under such circumstances, what could an eighteen-year-old do but try to rationalise her sufferings in the terms of fate and destiny[8]:

> I console my mind
> By this account
> Fate is the cause
> Of all these sorrows
>
> or
>
> Strides of Fate
> Utterly unstoppable
> Why to fret over it
> Pointlessly.

However, no matter whether you blame it on fate or something else, there might come a point when it becomes impossible to bear any more pain - mental and/or physical, as it happened with Bahinabai:

> Now I feel like
> Setting myself on fire
> Or strike my head
> With a saw
>
> Feel like hurling
> Myself into the river
> Or just wander off
> Beyond the horizon.

It is the great fortune of Maharashtra that Bahinabai was not compelled to act upon these thoughts, but there should not be an iota of doubt in anyone's mind that it was only her steely nerves and her unshakeable devotion that saw her through this unimaginable trauma. All that unthinkable suffering on one hand and its magnificently restrained expression on the other hand - I have no compunction about admitting that I fail to comprehend the height of Bahinabai's artistic genius.

Bahinabai: The Social Commentator

Bahinabai's autobiography does not stop at documenting her personal life alone; in its course, it lays bare many social evils prevalent at her times. For, in Bahinabai's case, unfortunately, these social evils were part and parcel of her own personal life. It all starts with the child marriage that she is subjected to as a toddler. In her account of this marriage, Bahinabai - in her signature calm and composed voice - makes a very strong statement as she denounces her husband's learning for marrying a three-year-old at the age of 30:

> Widower he was
> Thirty years old
> My blessed husband
> A learned man.

Despite her very restrained tone, one can understand how loaded these lines are when one bears in mind the fact that her "learned" husband would have been 40ish and Bahinabai 13ish at the time of consummating their marriage. Whatever might their reasons have been to marry off their daughter so cursorily, Bahinabai's parents also appear to be the victims of the prevalent societal norms, having to overspend for the extravagant wedding and the crushing dowry, getting buried under insurmountable debts:

> Over four days lasted
> The wedding celebrations
> Couldn't understand at all
> Lord's intents
>
> Dear parents mine
> Stricken with poverty
> Under this burden
> Got smothered[9].

Apparently, it was this debt that Bahinabai's father could not repay in the coming years, forcing the entire family to flee their native place. Although she does not say it in as many words, it was this marriage that resulted in uprooting of her entire family, making them go door-to-door in search of their daily bread.

In this autobiography, we also get to see how the patriarchal forces manage to subjugate such a rebellious woman as Bahinabai by all means possible and to the fullest extent. When he is not able to make Bahinabai dance to his tunes by the means of brutal beating, Bahinabai's husband uses the typical patriarchal weapon against her, threatening to abandon her. As intended, this threat comes down upon her as a mighty blow that crushes her rebellion and she is left with no option but to surrender at his feet:

> Service to my husband
> He is my only god
> My husband is for me
> The Being Supreme
>
> Water from his feet
> Be all the holy waters
> Without that water
> Rest is futile.

Her spirit is so thoroughly crushed and her surrender is so absolute that one fails to imagine the extent of helplessness of this teenager when she says:

> My husband is life
> And I am the body
> My husband is all the good
> That happened to me.

This suppression of her spirit apparently does not stop even after absolute surrender and exacts thorough purgation of the prior beliefs in Bahinabai, making her profess:

> Vitthal is of rocks
> Tuka is of dreams
> Why should I keep
> From the real bliss?

This process of mental subjugation of the woman in question gets complete only upon her unconditional acceptance of the very ideology that she had challenged in the first place:

> I will partake infinite
> This bliss in service
> This is what the Vedas too
> Expect of me.

Interestingly, we also get to see the forces of caste-hegemony in action when Bahinabai and her family arrive in Dehu, Tukaram's village. Bahinabai's autobiography is historically significant in this regard too, since there are no first person accounts of the ways in which caste-hegemony is imposed upon those who try to challenge it, until the Marathi dalit autobiographies of the latter half of the twentieth century appear on the literary horizon. Although not from the perspective of a dalit, in Bahinabai's autobiography, we get to see this evil power at work in the form of Mambaji when he threatens Bahinabai's husband for not becoming his follower:

> I will get you banished
> From the ranks of the brahmins
> Don't you dare to talk to me
> Of devotion to Guru.

We also get an insight into how these threats of excommunication were executed socially in this interaction between Bahinabai and Mambaji:

> Then he said to me,
> I don't know your caste
> So I will consider you
> As shudras

Are you of goldsmiths
Or *golak* by caste
You have no privileges
Of the brahmins

If you ever go to have food
Anywhere as such a privilege
I will drag you all then
To the court of law.

It is so sickening to know how the existing legal system was used by these caste-supremacists to maintain their hold over the entire social machinery.

Mambaji's letter to the higher authorities, complaining against Tukaram and Bahinabai, also makes a fine example of these universal machinations in the name of protecting the "true religion":

He performs kirtan
In the temple all the time
Even the brahmins fall
At his feet
…
Grievous threat I perceive
To true religion in all this
Therefore I am sending
This dispatch
…
Quackery pretentious
Threatens true religion
It must be protected
O chief of lords.

To Bahinabai's credit, she gives us an account of all these happenings as objectively as possible, as if she was very well aware of her responsibilities as an honest documenter of her times.

Bahinabai & Tukaram and Their Contemporaries

Seventeenth century was the century that changed the course of Maharashtra's history – socially, politically and culturally. It was the century of two of the greatest people to have ever been born in this land - Sant Tukaram and Chhatrapati Shivaji. An autobiography written in that century could have been seldomly written without documenting the times of either or both of them. Chhatrapati Shivaji had just laid the foundation of the Swarajya by conquering Torna Fort in the year Bahinabai arrived in Dehu with her family (1646), so we find absolutely no mention of him in her extant autobiography, although she outlived him. However, the sole purpose of her arrival in Dehu was to meet Tukaram, and not only does she meet him but she also documents all the possible happenings around Tukaram during her stay there, thus making her autobiography a first-rate resource to know and to understand Tukaram.

Such was Bahinabai's devotion towards Tukaram that even before having seen/met him ever, she had declared:

> Baheni says Tuka
>
> Is my Guru, my brother.

Soon her devotion reaches to the point where Tukaram replaces the Lord in her prayers:

> Pandurang is Tukaram
>
> Pandurang is Tukaram
>
> How can they be separated
>
> From each other?

However, she is not expressing only her belief here but echoing the masses of her times, too, when she declares Tukaram to be Pandurang:

> Baheni says all
> People proclaimed,
> Tukoba manifestly
> Pandurang.

Along with the abhang of Tuakram's younger brother Kanhoba, Bahinabai's autobiography is the crucial contemporary document to understand Tukaram's final years and in the context of the stanza quoted above, it is enlightening to remember one of Tukaram's final abhang here:

> People consider me god
> Such a sacrilegious deed
>
> Now do as you deem right
> My head in your hand, and knife
>
> Right I have none
> To be worshipped thus
>
> Mind recognises sin
> Tuka says, O my parents[10].

Evidently, Tukaram was not happy at all with people treating him as a/the god and this must have proved pivotal in his consequent departure on a pilgrimage with no intention to return. Instead of speculating such baseless theories as Tukaram being murdered to replace equally unacceptable theories like bodily ascension to heaven, it is high time that we find our way with the help of such contemporary accounts such as Kanhoba's elegiac abhang written right after Tukaram's departure. Unfortunately, Bahinabai's extant autobiography stops just short of revealing what transpired in those fateful days. She was present in Dehu during Tuakaram's final days there, and it is not possible that she would not have documented something as monumental as Tukaram's departure. Rather than propagating unsubstantiated theories, locating that copy of *Bahinabai's Gatha* which has this part of her autobiography will be a true contribution to Tukaram studies.

Bahinabai Had a Little Calf!

If you heard an echo of a nursery rhyme in the line above, then you are not mistaken, this is indeed going to be a bit of a literary curio. When the first time I read Bahinabai's account of her calf accompanying her everywhere including to the place of scripture-reading, I was delighted to remember "Mary had a little lamb":

> Along with them
> I would go for listening
> The calf too would go
> Along with us
>
> I would sit there
> Near my mother
> The calf too running
> Would stand beside.

A little digging up on the internet added to my delight further, knowing that it was a poem composed by the American Sarah Joseph Hale, published in 1830, which is based on a true event that Hale witnessed as a teacher. A student of hers actually was accompanied by her lamb one fine day and did not go away even after Sarah turned it out, owing to the commotion it caused in the class. Almost two centuries apart and with the proverbial seven seas separating them, an Indian and an American girl experiencing the same bond of love transcending species was a very reassuring experience for me.

Bahinabai's Imagery

Without further ado, let me confess here - if it has not been written all over this introduction already - that I am thoroughly fascinated by all of the Varkari poets. So great is this fascination that it has withstood all my university education in English literature and all the reading of the world literature that accompanied it, and today I find Varkari poetry to be of the highest literary order, comparable to the greatest poetries of the world. And among all of the Varkari poets, I am particularly drawn towards *Bahinabai's Gatha* for its multifacetedness which I will continue to explore. An important characteristic of good poetry is its imagery and here I would like to present just a few of my favourite images from Bahinabai's autobiography. Bahinabai's images are such an integral part of her narrative that sometimes it is almost impossible to distinguish between the two. For example, she uses a very exquisite image while describing the difficulties that her family faced on fleeing their native place. Standing on the bank of the Godavari, they could not go back to Devgaon, but moving forward into the unknown seemed equally daunting. No wonder, they found:

> The river was flooded
> On both the banks.

Further down the narrative, Bahinabai again faces a dilemma when she finds her married life becoming an obstacle in her spiritual path. This must have been a very tormenting experience for the conventionally brought-up Bahinabai as she was drawn towards two opposing goals with equal might. It is at this point that she uses one of the most inspired images that I have ever come across. Unable to decide between the two options before her - pursuing the spiritual path abandoning her married life like Mirabai did or continuing her married life abandoning her ever increasing spiritual aspirations like the scores of other women did - and with the compulsion to choose between the two, she cries out:

> Cobra at the door
> House engulfed in fire
> How to save one's life
> In such an event?

Finally, for the sake of perspective, I would again like to take you back to England but this time in the year 1818 when on 27th February, a certain John Keats wrote to his publisher John Taylor:

> "But it is easier to think what poetry should be, than to write it, and this leads me to another axiom. That if poetry comes not as naturally as the leaves to a tree, it had better not come at all"[11].

Keats has used some of the greatest images ever committed to paper but I find this image drawing a comparison between writing of poetry and sprouting of leaves to be the most beautiful. It seems that the great minds do not just think alike but they think in similar images too, because Bahinabai has described her process of writing poetry using a very similar image:

> Baheni says my mind
> Began to compose
> Like the sea advances
> With the moon in the sky.

Bahinabai and the Abhang Form

A very distinct feature of the Varkari tradition of Maharashtra has been the composition of the abhang which are essentially lyrics that can also be employed for narrative purposes, among others. Origins of the abhang are murkier but one finds the most diverse explorations of this form in *Sant Danyandev's Gatha*, whereas the most accomplished practitioner of this form is known to be Sant Tukaram. In its most widely used forms, an abhang comprises either two-lined stanzas or four-lined stanzas. Four-lined stanzas have three hexasyllabic lines and the last line has four syllables, while the line length in two-lined stanzas varies greatly. Further, two-lined stanzas are rhyming couplets, while four-line stanzas have mostly *abbc* rhyme scheme but also can have *aaab* rhyme scheme occasionally. However, these two stanza-forms are never used together in the same abhang, in other words, an abhang is always composed entirely in either four-lined or two-lined stanza form. Generally, an abhang consists of a minimum of four stanzas with no upper limit on the number of stanzas. Basically, an abhang provides immense freedom of movement and expression to the poet, hence their popularity. Bahinabai has preferred the four-lined stanza form for her autobiography and also for her translation of the *Vajrasuchi Upanishad*. In doing so, Bahinabai has made noteworthy contributions towards expanding the horizons of the abhang form as she happens to be the first saint-poet to use the abhang form to translate an entire Sanskrit text into Marathi.

If the abhang seem to be so simple in their composition, why do they appear to be so difficult to read? Even after mastering the Old Marathi, why do people struggle in understanding the abhang? The main reasons are that the abhang do not employ punctuation marks and the interrelationship between and/or among the words in a line is not determined only by the laws of syntax, demanding a great deal of effort on the part of the reader in the process of signification. Additionally, most of the abhang employ end-stop lines but some use enjambment, too. This makes the situation especially trickier in the absence of punctuation marks with no guidance provided for the reader as to whether to stop reading at the end of the line or to run on to the next. In other words, the Marathi abhang are the quintessential writerly text in the Barthesian sense.

Naturally, ambiguity abounds, as it is supposed to in any good poetry, in the abhang. Let's understand this better with an example from Bahinabai's autobiography where she is narrating her initiation at the hands of Tukaram in her dream:

> I placed my head
> On his feet earnestly
> He gave me the text
> Mantra Gita.

These happen to be the most debated lines in *Bahinabai's Gatha*, since there is no comma between Mantra and Gita in the source, which leaves it open to multiple interpretations: What was given to Bahinabai? A text called "Mantra Gita" or the mantra (Ram Krushna Hari) and *The Gita*? Or was it three things? However, adding a comma here will rob this abhang off this significant (in the semantic sense of this word) ambiguity it carries. Therefore, here and in all my translations of other abhang, I have used punctuations only when I could not do away with them altogether without affecting signification. For example, I have used a comma to indicate the beginning of direct speech, but I have not used inverted commas. By doing so, I have tried to present the nearest version of the meaning-laden source text in my translation, instead of imposing my singular interpretation of that abhang on my reader.

Why & How do I Translate?

As someone who has managed to master English to some extent and is blessed enough to still have remained deeply rooted in his mother-culture, I consider it my foremost duty to take my literary heritage to the world in the language of the world. Marathi has one of the oldest literary traditions among all the modern languages of the world but, unfortunately, those who are deeply immersed in that tradition shy away from English, while those Marathi speakers who have the ability to express themselves in English lack the deep connection with that tradition, which is the prerequisite for a good translation of this kind. This realisation infinitely heightened my sense of duty towards my Varkari heritage and gave birth to the translator that I am today. It was with this realisation that I began to translate Varkari poets a decade ago and to commemorate the centenary year of Rabindranath Tagore's *One Hundred Poems of Kabir,* I published my first works of translation *One Hundred Poems of Tukaram* and *One Hundred Poems of Chokha Mela* in 2015. I chose this year not because I am a fan of Gurudev's translation (for me, paraphrasing cannot be termed as translation), but I understand the significance of his book of 1915: It was the first English translation of Bhakti literature by an Indian, to the best of my knowledge. Also, 1915 happens to be the year in which J. Nelson Fraser completed his *Poems of Tukaram,* making it a golden letter year for the translation of Bhakti literature in India.

Perhaps it is because I translate the poets whom I revere that I do not agree with the prevalent flagrant standpoint: A translator requires / possesses more creativity than the source writer. I also have very strong objections to the incestuous liberties that the translators are taking with the source text in the name of their pseudo-creativity. In fact, I firmly believe if you have so much creative juices flowing, why not go ahead and create something of your own? Why feast parasitically upon someone else's creation? This standpoint of mine should not be misinterpreted as assigning the translator's work and talents lesser significance. Quite contrarily, I believe that a good translator possesses the highest possible verbal intelligence and works as the bridge between minds that would not have come together ever otherwise. However, I refuse to weigh the source writer and the translator in the same scale simply because only one of them has the power to create something new and for me, even the best translation cannot be as considered as creating something new. When in doubt, I ask myself only this question: Can a translator even exist without a source writer?

For me, as a translator, the form of a poem is as important as its contents and the smallest unit of translation is the line in a stanza. Looking from this vantage point, I try to recreate the nearest possible English copy of the abhang at hand, line by line, stanza by stanza. If there are multiple interpretations possible, I try to retain those too in my translation. I would have loved to retain the rhyme scheme also, but such efforts proved to render the translation veering far off from its source, so I had to abandon rhymes in my translation. I am painfully aware of the fact that this approach of mine has resulted in some very awkward phrases and frequent contorted syntax, which may lie far away from natural English - some might even refuse to call it English at all - but that is the compromise I choose to make in order to remain semantically as loyal to my source as syntactically possible.

Navi Mumbai   Chandrakant Kaluram Mhatre

January 2023

      NOTES:

1.   I find it difficult to translate Marathi संत as "saint" in English, especially before the name of any particular individual, since these two terms are simply not analogous culturally. To be a "saint" one needs to be dead, performing miracles (after dying, too) is a must, and getting canonised by the Roman Catholic Church is paramount. This is not the same as *becoming* a sant solely on the merit of one's thoughts (as expressed in one's poems) and actions (as performed when alive). This might sound as hair-splitting to many and maybe it is, for such words are known to gain newer meanings over the time, so I may use "saint" in the general sense but while referring to any particular individual, I will stick to "Sant".

2.	Javadekar, Shalini. "Abhang 589, 590". *Sant Bahenabaincha Gatha,* Continental Prakashan, 1979, Pp. 457.

3.	Chitre, Dilip. "The Image of Vithoba". *Says Tuka,* Sontheimer Cultural Association, 2003, Pp. 69.

4.	कलियुगीं दोन वर्ण । शुद्र आणि ब्राम्हण
	"In the Kaliyuga, there are only two varnas:
	The shudras and the brahmins".

This was the dictum coined by the caste-brahmins during the mediaeval times in Maharashtra. It was by this illogical logic, that the caste-brahmins could declare even the Mahajan of the village to be a shudra, as it happened with Sant Tukaram. Despite being born in a farmer family (vaishya), he was labelled and treated as a shudra in accordance with the above-mentioned dictum.

5.	I am well aware of the controversy around Ashvaghosha's authorship of *Vajrasuchi,* however for the sake of keeping the arguments readily accessible, I am not going down that rabbit hole here.

6.	मूलग्रंथिचेया संस्कृता । सर्वें नीट मऱ्हाटी पढतां ।

अभिप्रायें मानलेया उचिता । कवणि भूमिका ते नेणवे ॥४२॥ अध्याय १०

(*Dnyanadevi, Vol. 2.* Mumbai University, 1994, Pp. 582)

7.	These lines keep reminding me of Harivansh Rai Bachchan:
	वेद-लोकाचार प्रहरी/ताकते हर चाल मेरी
	बद्ध इस वातावरण में/क्या करे अभिलाष यौवन!

(*Madhukalash,* Rajpal & Sons, 2018, Pp. 36)

8.   One comes across similar fatalistic, and equally poignant, rationalisation to make sense of one's unending sufferings in Chokha Mela's abhang:

> Now I am not angry
> With anyone, O Lord
> I have accepted
> My own fate.

(*One Hundred Poems of Chokha Mela*, Runaal Publications, 2015, Pp. 32)

9.   This is one of those abhang that appear only in Kolharkar Text. Given its highly critical tone, it is understandable that it was expunged from the Shiur manuscript which Umarkhane has relied upon. It is the inclusion of such significant abhang that makes me consider Kolharkar Text to be the authoritative extant text of Bahinambai's poems.

10.   Mhatre, Chandrakant. *One Hundred Poems of Tukaram*, Runaal Publications, 2015, Pp. 32

11.   Keats, John. *Selected Letters of John Keats*, Harvard University Press, 2002, Pp. 97

ಞಞಞ || **1** || ಜಜಜ

Devgaon is the place
Of my parents, dear friend
To the East of which
Verul[1] lies

All of the deities
Assembled wherein
That be the place
Devgaon

On his journey
From the Himalayas
Agasti[2] resided where
During chaturmas[3]

To the west of it
Flows the Shivnadi
Among all holy waters
It's extraordinary

Millions of holy waters
Converge wherein
Lakshayani[4] resides there
All the while

Perceiving its sanctity
Agasti frequented the place
To perform rituals
At sunrise

Agasti has bestowed
A boon on Lakshagram
Million holy waters
Exist therein

Bathing, giving alms there
Performing rituals
Blessed would be that man
Know this well

Residing at Devgaon
Agasti himself
Bathed in the Shivnadi
All the while

Baheni says such
Is the place Devgaon
It is the place
Of my birth

1. Verul (वेरूळ) - Mispronounced as Ellora by the colonial British. One of the largest rock-cut temple-monastery complexes in the world. About 20 km from Bahinabai's Devgaon.
2. Agasti (अगस्ती) - Also known as Agastya, a prominent Vedic sage who travelled the entire length of Indian subcontinent, acting as a link between the north and the south
3. Chaturmas (चातुर्मास) - The holiest period in the Indian calendar, roughly corresponding with mid-June to mid-October of the Gregorian calendar, literally meaning 'four months'.
4. Lakshayani (लाक्षायणी) Residing deity of Lakhani village, approx. 6 km to the west of Bahinabai's Devgaon

ಅಞಞ || **2** || ಜಜಜ

Devgaon is the place*
Of my parents, dear friend
Branch Wajesani
Maunas clan

In such a family
I was born
To manifest the path
In feminine form

That family had
No bhakti lineage
Never indulged in listening
To holy scriptures

Baheni says the birth
Mind's aspirations
Such is this enigma
Known to Narayan

* This abhang is one of those which are found only in the Kolharkar Text. First two lines of this abhang are exactly the same as the previous abhang, but the remaining 14 lines are very different in tone and style from the previous abhang.

ಐಐಐ || **3** || ಜುಜುಜು

Aauji Kulkarni
Scribe in that place
In his family
I was born

Mother Janaki
Father Aaudev
Named as Devgaon
Is their place

In their family
They had no children
For the sake of children
They strove

Taking holy dips
At Lakshagram regularly
Worship of Lord Shiva
They commenced

After many days
A dream occurred
To my dear father
To Aauji

You'll beget two children
A daughter and a son
A holy brahmin
Told him

Baheni says within a year
I was conceived
After full nine months
A daughter was born

● ∾ ঙ ●

ఆఆఆ || **4** || బుబుబు

There were celebrations
For naming ceremony
Brahmins were treated
With a feast

Father Aaudev
Went to the forest
When all of a sudden
There was a gain

A gold coin wrapped
In yellow silk cloth
Was found on the way
To Verul

Returning home
He spoke joyfully
Daughter has brought us
Good luck

Vireshwar brahmin
Astrologer precise

My horoscope
He had drawn

Great fortunes
She will bring to you
Thus he interpreted
The horoscope

Devout she will be
For blessed she is
Long life is bestowed
Upon her

Baheni says thus
Predicted the brahmin
He was gifted with
Clothing and cows

●~ల్ళ~●

ఴఴఴ || **5** || ಐಐಐ

Other girls would play
With pretend toys
I would prefer to chant
Lord's name

Other childish games
I disliked as well
Whence came self-assurance
I never knew

Disliked frolicking
Or dancing with sticks*
I would rather
Sit still

Baheni says all
Was predestined
That took course
In this life

● ᰡ ᰢ ●

*A girls' dance, generally in a circle, with a stick in each of the hands, striking the sticks alternately against their partners' while moving around rhythmically with or without the beats of drums. Called *tiparya* (टिपऱ्या) in Marathi, suggestive of the sound the striking sticks make.

ఴఴఴ || **6** || ಜಜಜ

Brahmins would arrive
With the intention
Of seeking my hand
In marriage
Then unexpectedly
As destined to be
A family friend arrived
From Shiur

A distant relative
Desirous of marriage

Righteous, a gem of a man
Named Pathak

He proposed marriage
Engagement took place
Wedding was arranged
In due course

Then was born
My younger brother
Blessing of the worship
Of yore

Harbinger of good luck
They called me
For having younger brother
I was praised

Baheni says thus
I grew three years old
What happened next
I will narrate

● ෴ ●

ಅಅಅ || **7** || ಜಜಜ

My father belongs
To the great Maunas clan
From the revered Gautam clan
My husband*

An astrologer
Based in Shivpur
My parents gave me
In marriage to him

Widower he was
Thirty years old
My blessed husband
A learned man

Baheni says in marriage
To him I was given away
Dowry was given
Of all kinds

● ❦ ❧ ●

*This throws light on the heartless inner workings of the caste system in India - not only there are castes and subcastes that consider themselves superior to others; but even within a subcaste, there are clans (गोत्र) that consider themselves superior to others! For example, Gautam clan is considered to be of much higher social standing than the Maunas clan. It was perhaps this social-climbing   on part of Bahinabai's parents that led them to marry off their three years old daughter to a 30-year-old widower.

ॐॐॐ || **8** || ཨུཨུཨུ

My dear parents
Arranged the marriage
I was given away
In Gautam clan

9

Over four days lasted
Wedding celebrations
Can't understand at all
Lord's intents

Dear parents mine
Stricken with poverty
Under this burden
Got smothered

We fled the land
Fearing inheritance feud
The river was flooded
On both the banks

Taking with us
My husband
Travelled far away
To Lord Shiva's[1]

With my parents
Brother and husband
Baheni says settled there
For a while

1.	Kaigaon-Toka situated at 48km South of Bahinabai's Devgaon. Famous for the confluence of rivers Godavari and Pravara as well as a number of ancient temples of Lord Shiva, including the Siddheshwar temple.

ಐಐಐ || **9** || ಜಜಜ

Four years after
Marriage was solemnised
An enmity ensued between
My father and his kin

Owing to inheritance
Bitter feuds began
My father sent for
My husband

Pay off all the debts
Of the kith and kin
They are laying claim to
All my land

Now from here
We must go far away
Then only we will
Find peace

You are our beloved
Son-in-law, our friend
Pray, make us suffer not
Thus anymore

We are imprisoned
With no one to help
You be our saviour
Rescue us

Then my husband
Got us out of there
Right in the pitch dark
Of midnight

He took my parents
My brother along with me
Travelling in the dead of night
To the banks of Godavari

At the confluence of Pravara
We took holy dips
Visited the temple
Of Siddhanath*

Baheni says onwards
We moved from there
Having touched the feet
Of Lord Shiva

●⸱ఴౡ⸱●

*Another name of Lord Shiva, variant of *Siddheshwar*

ఆఆఆ || **10** || ಜಜಜ

Having seen Godavari
Lord Siddheshwar
Didn't feel like
Going away

Thanks to inclination
And upbringing
One loves to listen
To Lord's praise

Listening to scripture-reading
Visiting places of worship
Serving the brahmin[1]
One loves

Hermits and the good
Saints and Mahanubhav[2]
Craves for their company
My mind

Leaving such a place
Pains me deeply
Such a misfortune
What to do

Baheni says onwards
Away from Lord Shiva's
My husband took us
With great pleasure

1.   For Bahinabai a 'brahmin' was not defined by his caste. For
Bahinabai's definition of the brahmin, please see her translation of *Vajrasuchi
Upanishad* in Appendix I.

2.   Mahanubhav (महानुभाव) - Another Krishna-worshipping sect,
contemporaneous with and comparable to the Varkari sect in some of its
tenets, such as indiscrimination on the basis of caste, class, creed or gender.

ಆಉಆ || **11** || ಜುಜುಜು

Asking for alms
We journeyed on
Facing hardships
Of all kinds

Along with parents
Brother and husband
Visited the woods
Of Lord Shiva

After duly beholding
Lord Narsimha[1]
We visited the place
Of Lord Pandurang[2]

River Chandrabhaga[3]
Pundalik[4] revered
Sound of the flute[5]
That liberates all

Holy dip in Padmale[6]
Beholding the Lord
Listening to the praise
Of the Lord

Rahi, Rakhumai
Satyabhama[7] and all
Beheld everything
Via Eastern entrance

Stepping inside the temple
From the grand gateway
Filled the mind
With great bliss

Beholding the divine
Form of Pandurang
Satiated the eyes
All the senses

Circumnavigated the Lord
Filled with great bliss
Making the mind free
Of all desires

Felt so strongly
To settle in that place
But it was not
Destined to be

Better to die instantly
Than to leave Pandhari[8]
Didn't wish to leave
The holy waters

Baheni says in Pandhari
We stayed five nights
Owing to our
Great fortune

● ৵৩৹ ●

1.	Narsimha (नरसिंह) - Fourth incarnation of Lord Vishnu, half man (*Nar*), half lion (*Simha*). The temple that Bahinabai visited is situated in Nira-Narsingpur in Pune District, about 270 km from Bahinabai's Devgaon

2.	Pandurang (पांडुरंग) - Principal deity of the Varkari sect to which Bahinabai belonged, also known as Vitthal, Vithoba, Pandharinath. The temple is situated in Pandharpur in Solapur District, more than 300 km from Bahinabai's Devgaon

3.	Chandrabhaga (चंद्रभागा) - River Bhima takes a crescent shape when it flows by Pandharpur, hence the name Chandrabhaga i.e. Crescent shaped

4.	Pundalik (पुंडलिक) - Varkaris believe that it was owing to Pundalik's devotion that Lord Krishna reincarnated Himself as Vitthal in Pandharpur. Pundalik's temple is situated on the bank of Chandrabhaga and every Varkari who visits Pandharpur pays obeisance to Pundalik by visiting his temple.

5.	Lord Vitthal (विठ्ठल), being reincarnation of Lord Krishna, retains some of his traits, one of them being playing the flute

6.	Padmale (पद्माळे) - A sacred lake in Pandharpur, also known as Padmavati lake

7.	Rahi (राही), Rakhumai (रखुमाई), Satyabhama (सत्यभामा) - Lord Vitthal's consorts who are also worshipped by the Varkaris. Rakhumai stands for Mother Rukmini and Rahi stands for Radha

8.	Pandhari (पंढरी) - Another name for Pandharpur

ఞఞఞ || **12** || ಹಹಹ

On Chaitra[1] Pornima[2]
We went to Lord Shiva's[3]
Visited the Lord
Undertook the pilgrimage

Became content
On beholding the Lord

Prayed for his grace
Devoutly

Five nights there
Having stayed
We went further
To Shinganapur

Received raw grains
Readily in alms
That would fill my mind
With happiness[4]

Sweet as nectar
Would taste that food
All sins would be destroyed
On consuming it

Baheni says then
I attained age of nine
Narrated circumstances
Thus far

●⤫⤬●

1.   Chaitra (चैत्र) - First month of Indian lunar calendar, coincides roughly with mid-March to mid-April

2.   Pornima (पोर्णिमा) - Full-moon

3.   Shikhar-Shinganapur (शिखर-शिंगणापूर), situated in Satara district, about 85 km to the west of Pandharpur

4.   Asking for alms (*bhiksha*) was considered a sacred rite and the recipient of alms (*bhikshuk*) was looked up to as a holy man.

ಆಉಆಉ || **13** || ಜಉಜಉ

My husband asked us
For our counsel
No shelter here
We have any

We should settle down
In some brahmin village
I feel it strongly
In my heart

Rahimatpur[1] has
Brahmin populace
We should stay
In that place

Baheni says all
That is predestined
Isn't left behind
On change of place

●~ೞ~ఞ~●

1.   Rahimatpur (रहिमतपूर) - A small town in Satara district, about 70 km
             to the west of Shikhar-Shinganapur

ಆಉಆಉ || **14** || ಜಉಜಉ

All settled down
In Rahimatpur
All of us began
To ask for alms

My husband performed
Great deal of rituals
God blessed him
With His grace

The village-priest
Of that place
Longed to visit
Varanasi

To perform on his behalf
His official duties
He promptly deputed
My husband

While I am gone
On a pilgrimage to Varanasi
Ratnakar[1], the astrologer, be
The village-priest

Having found aptly
Such a learned scholar
He handed over
All hi s charge

My husband consented
And we stayed there
For one entire year
Was taken care of

When he returned
To the village
He sheltered us
For another year

By that time
I was eleven
I wished for
Company of saints

I wished to listen
To the reading of scriptures
Serving brahmins
My mind longed for

However, the fate
Pulled us out of there
Leaving behind that place
We moved on

Mind was dispirited
Disliked everything
But there is no fighting
With the fate

Baheni says onwards
Holy place of Kolhapur
Immensely sacred
We visited

●❧❧●

1.   Ratnakar (रत्नाकर) - This seems to be how Bahinabai's husband was commonly known as, although he was officially named as Gangadhar Pathak.

ଔଔଔ || **15** || ଊଊଊ

Went to Pandhari[1]
From the Lord Shiva's
Beholding saints
Experienced joy

Companionship of the saints
Dearer than life
But I was scared
Of my husband

Jamadagni's[2] wrath
I had heard of
My husband was
His living image

Bahini says thus
I became of eleven
Not a moment of joy
For my mind

●๏๏●

1.   Two years spent in the company of the caste brahmins don't seem to count for Bahinabai, hence this wishful thinking of traveling from Shikhar-Shinganapur to Pandharpur while in reality they travelled from Rahimatpur to Kolhapur.

2.　　Jamadagni (जमदग्नी) - One of the most revered Seven Sages (*saptarshi*) and father to Vishnu's sixth incarnation, Lord Parashuram. Jamadagni, according to the legend, in a fit of rage, ordered the execution of his wife Renuka and turned his four sons to stone when they refused to oblige.

ೞೞೞ ‖ **16** ‖ ೞೞೞ

Hirambhat one there[1]
Brahmin learned in Vedas
Well-versed in both branches[2]
Of Yajurveda

Great man of fortune
Performer of yajnas
A number of students
Studied there

In his house
We sought shelter
The stay restful there
Listening to their chanting

Jayram Gosavi there
Would read holy texts
We would always attend
Reading of Bhagwat[3]

Baheni says there
I settled down
Ever engrossed with
The Truth Supreme

1.   At Kolhapur, situated about 120 km to the South of Rahimatpur

2.   *Yajurveda* exists in the form of two Samhitas: One which is well-organised and includes Shatapatha Brahmana (शतपथ ब्राम्हण), a prose text describing Vedic rituals, is called *Shukla Yajurveda* and the other, less-organised and without Brahmana is called *Krishna Yajurveda.*

3.   *Bhagwat* (भागवत) - One of the eighteen great puranas

ಙಙಙ || **17** || ಶಜಶಜ

Husband would conduct rites
For the sake of livelihood
How to expect the Lord
To be there

Scholars of Vedas
Tend to dislike bhakti
Being dependent
I was helpless

Tender of age
Considered puerile
In the terror of Vedas
Rendered silent

Baheni says mine
Mind agonises
Tortured exceedingly
By this life

●੭੭●

ಅಞಞ || **18** || ಜಜಜ

Chanting Lord's name
Was forbidden at my home
Knowledge of the Gita was enemy
For my family

A disliking for the Lord
Undertaking pilgrimage
I was married off
In such a family

Company of the saints
Worship of the Lord
Listening to the scriptures
Disliked all

Baheni says sins
Thus accumulated mine
Let them be destroyed
To calm my mind

●⤙⤚●

ಅಞಞ || **19** || ಜಜಜ

All the Vedas call out
The Puranas clamour
In the company of a woman
Nothing to gain

I am nothing
But a woman's body
How do I find now
The Path Supreme?

Idiocy, affection
Enchantment deceptive
The company of a woman
Just calamitous

Baheni says such
Calamitous woman's body
How do I walk here
The Path Supreme?

●⚭⚮●

ങങങ ‖ **20** ‖ ಜಜಜ

A woman's body
Dependent existence
The measure of detachment
Holds no sway

Such deprivation
Thanks to the mores
Why did the Lord
Create me?

Body is seared
By three afflictions[1]

My mind considers
Ending life

Unable to serve the Lord
Even for a moment
All the near and dear ones
My adversaries

Bodily pleasures
Seem like enemies
Now who will look after
My wellbeing?

Baheni says just like
The thrown-up vomit
All of this world
Appears to me

●⚬⚬●

1. *Adhyatmik* (अध्यात्मिक) - caused by one's own body and mind, *adhibhautik* (अधिभौतिक) - caused by other beings, *adhidaivik* (आधिदैविक) - caused by natural calamities

---

೧೮೦೮ || **21** || ೱೞೞೞ

What sins committed
During previous lives
That I am separated now
From the Lord?

Borne as a human though
In the form of a woman
Seems to be culmination
Of uncountable sins

Deprived of the right
To studying scriptures
Gayatri is hidden away
By the brahmins

Must not articulate
The sounds of *Omkar*
Must not hear at all
Chanting of mantras

Must not speak a word
With another man
My husband is the image
Of Jamadagni

Baheni says mind
Gets smothered
The Lord too shows me
No mercy

● ⌘ ●

ಇಂಇಂ || **22** || ಜಜಜ

My being has undergone
So much of anguish
Immeasurably miserable
I've become, dear Lord

I console my mind
By this account
Fate is the cause
Of all these sorrows

Likes of Lord Brahma
Can't escape sorrows destined
What of the other tramps
In front of it?

Baheni says this
Is my being's fate
How can the Lord
Help me?

ಇಂಇಂ || **23** || ಜಜಜ

This body is but destined
To bear joys and sorrows
Have to undergo those
Necessarily

My accumulated sins
Are thus on the wane
I consider this to be
Indeed a gain

Mind longs for
Serving the Lord
Body is but tormented
By great pain

Baheni says such
If my destiny
Who can rid me
Of this pain?

|| 24 ||

Strides of Fate
Utterly unstoppable
Why to fret over it
Pointlessly

Have determined now
To hold steadfast
The Lord in mind
Pandurang

Afflictions of the body
No one can eliminate

This, O dear Lord
I came to realise

Baheni says now
I supplicate before you
Do not test my mind
O dear Lord

●⤳⤲●

ఴఴఴ || **25** || ಙಙಙ

My parents and brother are
Enamoured by material existence
They suffer colossal pain
In my company

Talking to You, o Lord
You understand me
I've got no one else
To speak of this

No one to guide me
On the path of salvation
I have no company
Of the good

I am on my own
Lost in the wilderness
Thirst and hunger
Remember not

I don't feel like
Talking to anyone
Please think about this
O dear Lord

Baheni says You
Alone I know of
Whom else should I
Tell all this?

● ❦ ●

❦ || **26** || ❦

My brother, my companion
You alone, my Lord
Saviour of the wretched
O Pandurang

I wish to worship you
Perform wifely duties too
How to achieve this
Tell me, o Lord

Adversarial to Vedas
Not the Path Supreme
Therefore I ask You
Tell me of this

Baheni says both
I wish to accomplish
Way to attain this
Tell me promptly

●~ఌఞ~●

ఒఒఒ || **27** || ಐಐಐ

Origin of detachment
Renouncing worldly matters
Forced to choose between
Home or hills

Such is my predicament
Rush swiftly, O Lord
With counsel conscientious
Guide my mind

Deserting husband
Is against the Vedas
The Path Supreme otherwise
Cannot attain

Cobra at the door
House engulfed in fire
How to save one's life
In such an event?

The Vedas proclaim
Do not abandon duties

But serving the Lord
Is what I love

Baheni says such
Obstacles mounting
How the agony deepens
Can't express

●~❧~●

❀❀❀ || **28** || ❀❀❀

Filled with penitence
Mind suffers immensely
Why dear Lord has
No mercy for me?

Now I feel like
Setting myself on fire
Or strike my head
With a saw

Feel like hurling
Myself into the river
Or just wander off
Beyond the horizon

Feel like sitting steadfast
Deep in the forest
Set out on a fast
Never to break

Baheni says my mind
Writhes in anguish
Why have you forsaken me
O dear Lord?

●❧ॐ❧●

ఇఇఇ || **29** || ಜಜಜಜ

Like the deer fallen
Into the trap
Like the blind lost
In the wilderness

Likewise became of me
Whom to ask for guidance?
My mind suffers thus
Endlessly

Fish without water
Calf without cow
Fawn without deer
Likewise

Baheni says, O Lord
Such tribulations
Cast a merciful glance
On the wretched

●❧ॐ❧●

ಞಞಞ || **30** || ಜಜಜ

On one occasion
When I was eighteen[1]
Great sacred observance
Fell on a Monday

Hirambhat received
A gift of a cow
The donor having seen
Her two-faced[2]

Black was that cow
Black was her calf
With due ceremony
Given away

Gold covered horns
Silver covered hooves
Draped with yellow
Silk cloth

According to the scriptures
Performed the gift of the cow
People flocked around
To witness it

Upon the birth of the calf
The cow was brought home
The calf began to feed
On her milk

Thus passed ten days
On the eleventh day
A brahmin spoke to Hirambhat
In his dream

You have sheltered
A brahmin in your house
Give away to him
This black cow

Just a dream it was
Still Hirambhat acted on it
Gave away the cow devoutly
To my husband

Our minds were filled
Naturally with joy
Opportunity we got
To serve the cow

Parents would regularly
Go to fetch fodder
Diligently served the cow
With great pleasure

That cow's calf
Was a female too
It developed affection
Great for me

The calf would feed
Only if I'd be around
Habituated to feed
In my presence

I would give water
I would give fodder
Without me restless
It would become

When I'd go to fetch water
It would call out to me
Along with its mother
Walk beside me

People seeing us
Would be amazed
Would keep observing
The cow and the calf

The calf was never
Kept tethered
Still it would not go
To the cow

It would eat the grass
Only if I would feed
It would drink water
Only if I gave

At night the calf
Would sleep next to me

Listening to the scriptures
It would grunt

It would accompany me
To listen to the scriptures
It would listen intently
Standing still

The cow would be in the shed
The calf at the scripture-reading[3]
When I went for holy dip
It accompanied me

People would wonder
It must be your kin
So many things
They would say

Some would say
The calf is a fallen sage
Some would say bad habits
Of this woman

Some would say
It must be indebted to her
On repaying her debts only
Be liberated

Whatever it be
The calf never left my side
I too grew very fond
Of the calf

Not seeing the calf
I would get restless
Fish without water
Feel likewise

Grinding or husking
Or fetching water
I disliked not having
The calf around

Short-tempered husband
Disapproved all this
But he felt pity
For me

Saying you have none
Children of your own
It's a good diversion
For your mind

You are so interested
In listening to the scriptures
Eager companion this
You have got
***
After some time
Jayram Gosavi
Arrived there
Fortuitously

Listening to scriptures
Serving the brahmin

Gifts for the learned
All began

He would read scriptures
At night, during day too
My parents loved
To attend it

Along with them
I would go for listening
The calf too would go
Along with us

I would sit there
Near my mother
The calf too running
Would stand beside

Wouldn't excrete or urinate
Would listen to kirtan[4]
The Lord's praise
With upright ears

After the ceremony of lamps
Everyone would bow down
The calf would place its head
On the ground

On seeing that
All people would laugh
But the kind at heart
Were pleased

Saying, fallen sage earlier
Must have been Lord's devotee
Reborn in the form of a calf
Behold

***

Then on one occasion
Moropant invited
Jayram Gosavi
To perform kirtan

On occasion of *Ekadashi*[5]
Late in the evening
Commenced ecstatically
The Lord's narrative

Jayram Gosavi
Took the dais
Amidst the multitude
Of his disciples

Commenced singing
Along with *taal*[6] and mridang
All of the people
Gathered there

I too was there
With my parents and brother
Listening to the narration
Blissfully

Accompanying me
The calf sat beside
Someone drove it
Out of the door

Saying there's no place
For people to sit
What's the use here
Of an animal?

I began to cry there
For the sake of the calf
Then it became known
To the Gosavi

The calf was bellowing
There I was crying
People told of this
To the Master

Saying, there is one girl
Staying at Hirambhat's
She has come here
For the kirtan

She always has
A calf with her
She takes it with her
Wherever she goes

Due to a lack of space
The calf was driven out

That has upset her
Hence crying

That calf is bellowing
Waiting outside
She is crying inside
Inconsolably

A mind reader
Swami Jayram
The calf's yearning
He recognized

Saying, bring it inside
In the form of a calf
Does the Omnipresent
Not reside?

It should not be called
By the name of an animal
Since it yearns
For the Lord's narrative

The calf was brought in
Was seated near dais
On seeing that
I was overjoyed

The great merciful
Spoke kindly to me too
Called me over
What a fortune!

Caressing both of us
Looked upon mercifully
Not bothered at all
By people's talk

The narrative resumed
With great enthusiasm
Fearless is the mind
Of the Vaishnav

Jayram Gosavi
Thus spoke further
Both of these are
Blessed truly

During the narrative
The calf stayed standing
Focused all faculties
While listening

This little girl
Is of tender age
Yet loves listening to scriptures
What a wonder!

Asked after me
Who accompanied there
My parents accompany me
He was told

Her husband is
Such a good match

But she is greatly inclined
To the worship of the Lord

Comes with her parents
To listen to the scriptures
Accompanied always
By the calf

Then I decided
On my own
And threw myself
At his feet

The calf likewise
Fell on his feet
What an amazement
For all the people

To his right and left
Both we were
He lifted up
Both of us

After the kirtan
People returned home
But it's unprecedented
They all said

Including Hirambhat
All the people
Wondered what would
All this mean

Baheni says thus
Happened in Kolhapur
What happened next
I will narrate

●~❀❀~●

1. Both Umarkhane and Kolhatkar texts give eleven (अकरा) as Bahinabai's age here, which is definitely a typo, since within a few months after this incident, Bahinabai and her family arrived in Dehu, which could not have been in 1939, given the timeline of Tukaram's life.
2. While the cow was giving birth to a calf. Donating such a cow along with the yet-to-be-born calf was considered to be one of the greatest good deeds (पुण्य).
3. Owing to the restrictions on the right to education as well as the paucity of books, public readings of the holy books were held, generally in temples but also at the private residences of the well-off.
4. Yet another popular form of devotional story-telling, interspersed with singing of devotional verses, accompanied by musical instruments viz. *Veena*, *Pakhwaj* and *Taal*.
5. Ekadashi (एकादशी) - Eleventh and twenty-sixth day of Indian lunar calendar, considered as very sacred
6. Taal (टाळ) - Cymbal-like palm-sized bell-bronze instrument

---

ଔଔଔ || **31** || ಜಜಜಜ

With parents and brother
Returned afterwards
To our place
With the calf

Two *ghatika*[2] night remained
When we arrived

Both the cow and the calf
Was fed

Hirambhat bathed
To perform fire-rites
Stars of *Kartik*[1] month
Shone in the sky

Morning chores
Performed, took bath
Caressed the horn
Of the cow

My husband too
Went for holy dip
Gaya of the South
Is Kolhapur
At that time
A certain Nirabai
Talked of the happenings
Of the night

She told my husband
What happened at the kirtan
She just meant to speak
Of the amazement

All about the calf
And also my crying
My husband's ears
Were infused with

Jayram Gosavi
Such a holy man
He blessed both of them
Caressing heads

What a fortune!
He spoke with them
Bestowed blessings
Befitting

Bhikshuk[3] by birth
Became very angry
He ran towards home
With great haste

Holding by plait
Beat me mercilessly
Hirambhat was distressed
Seeing that

Unstoppable, beating me
The cow bellowed
The calf too wailed
Grief-stricken

This all happened
When I was eleven
Had I fallen short
Fulfilling my duties?

My parents or brother
Didn't say anything

My husband controlled
His anger finally

When he calmed down
They asked him
Why so infuriated
With your wife?

He said, Yesternight
Disrepute brought upon me
During the kirtan
What a show of devotion!

What's in scripture-reading?
What's in the kirtan?
Thrashing is not at all
Unwarranted here
Having said this
He resumed beating
Unrestrained anger
Like raging fire

Baheni says at that time
I had no hope for life
Who can deliver from
What is predestined?

● ❧ ❧ ●

1. 1 ghatika (घटिका) = 24 minutes

2. Kartik (कार्तिक) - Seventh month of the Indian lunar calendar

3. Bhikshuk (भिक्षुक) - A caste brahmin who earns his livelihood by receiving alms (*bhiksha*), not to be confused with a beggar

---

ೞೞೞ || **32** || ಜಜಜ

You may torture my body
At my husband's hands
But my mind has made
This resolution

Won't cease Your worship
Even at the cost of my life
Now, O gracious Lord
Saviour of the wretched

Why do you test
My devotion thus?
I might meet my end
At my husband's hands

What should I do?
Such dilemma I face
It's not my body
I'm concerned with

Even if my body falls
My intent will survive
To behold Your Form Infinite
With enlightened eyes

To worship You
And perform my duties
To recognize You
Through the door of knowledge

Will my body survive
This kind of torment?
Why don't you listen to
My supplications?

If desire unfulfilled
Have to take rebirth
This dictum of the Vedas
I have heard of

Now in this calamity
My slaying be on You
You ought to protect
Your own child

Baheni says, O Lord
Why have you become
Deaf and blind too
O Preserver of the Universe?

ಞ‍ಞ‍ಞ || **33** || ‍ಞ‍ಞ‍ಞ

To his heart's content
He beat me rigorously
Tying my hands and legs
Threw me aside

Hirambhat told us
Get out of my house

This man seems to be
A murderer, a monster

Then my parents
Begged to Hirambhat
Pleading a great deal
Calmed him down

Saying, Allow us kindly
Just one more day
Tomorrow morning
We will depart

All that while
Both the calf and the cow
Did not eat at all
Nor drank water
Having seen the calf
And the cow's condition
My husband untied me
At that time

He brought me near
The cow and the calf
Began to whimper
Both of them

When I saw
The calf and the cow
I felt like
Better if I die

Baheni says he gave them
Fodder and water
But they did not take
Such great affection for me

● ৵ড় ●

ಐಐಐ || **34** || ಐಐಐ

Wouldn't eat fodder
Wouldn't take water
I too stopped
Taking food

Both wouldn't move
From their place
People would gather
To see them
People told of this
To Jayram Swami
To see the protestations
He too arrived

My husband greeted him
Reverently folding hands
I was still determined
In my mind

Seat was prepared
For Jayram Swami
Hirambhat received him
With great devotion

People gathered
To see the happenings
Jayram Swami at that time
Was delighted

He said, Brahmin
You are her husband
What I tell you now
Listen attentively

Very fortunate she is
Of mighty devotion
You must not bother her
By any means

By her own conviction
She will serve you well
She will attain salvation
As well

You must have performed
Great good deeds previously
Therefore, you have got
Such a spouse

The cow and the calf
Are her companions
Devoted to the Lord
Immersed in Oneness

She is her own Guru
She is her own means

She will break away
From all the bonds

Those who stay
In her company
They too will be blessed
With the joys of devotion

If you listen to me
You will fare well
Otherwise, what powers
Do I hold?

Baheni says Jayram
Having spoken thus
I could foresee all
Favourable signs

●♨♨●

ౠౠౠ || **35** || ಒಜುಜು

Jayram Swami then
Set off for his place
Along with the multitude
Of his disciples

Jayram told the disciples,
Steadfastly devoted
Are all these three
From previous birth

Some blemish earlier
In their devotion
Hence rebirth fortunate
In the bovine form

This girl is impeccable
In her devotion
Her mind has attained
Absolute purity

Conversation thus
Took place among them
That I overheard
Reverently

Baheni says then
Swami went to his place
Happenings of the past
I narrate

● ⁂ ●

ಜಜಜ || **36** || ಜಜಜ

Dwadashi[1] went by
Trayodashi[2] arrived
Final moments of the calf
Came nearer

At that time Hirambhat
Recited a shloka

Apt to the situation:
Mukam karoti[3]

Hardly had he recited
The first half of the shloka
When the calf
Began to speak

Yatkrupa tamaham vande
Uttering these words
The remaining shloka
The calf recited

All the people listened
To the remaining shloka
Spoke to each other
Astonished

Then the calf
Breathed its last
I went running
Towards it

I felt as if
I was dying
There is no altering
What is predestined

The cow bellowed
Hung up its neck
What an excruciating
Sound it was!

Baheni says my being
Was preserved by destiny
I do not know
What happened next

●❧❧●

1. Dwadashi - 12th or 27th day of a month in the Indian Lunar calendar
2. Trayodashi - 13th or 28th day of a month in the Indian Lunar calendar
3.   *Mukam karoti vachalam | pangum langhayate girim*
         The mute speak eloquently, the crippled scale mountains
         Yatkrupa tamaham vande | paramanand Madhavam
         when blessed by the Grace of the Lord, the manifestation of the Bliss
         Supreme; to Him I bow down devoutly.

———————————————————————

ಞಞಞ || **37** || ಜಜಜ

Soon the news
Reached Jayram Swami
That the calf had
Passed away

The calf breathed its last
Reciting half of the shloka
The highest form of knowledge
Couldn't hold a light

Then all the good
And the great devout
Singing Lord's praise
Carried the calf

On its final journey
Sacred flags escorted the calf
The cow accompanied
Disconsolate

Bellowing ceaselessly
Walked behind the procession
The cow's grief
Knew no bounds

Having buried the calf
People returned
After the ritual bath[1]
Went home

Going to the burial spot
The cow would wail
Then would turn back
For the home

She would observe me
But I laid unconscious
Signs of life in my body
None were found

Thus passed four days
Then it transpired
On the first day of the fortnight
At the midnight

A brahmin came forth
And spoke to me,

Stay watchful, lady
Act thoughtfully

Watchful, watchful
Be watchful of mind
My body trembled
On hearing him

The cow was not around
Nor the calf, nor people
I saw my dear mother
Seated before me

Brother and father
And husband sat around
A lamp was burning
Unblemished

Then I roused
My mind, made it watchful
Focusing it absolutely
On Lord's remembrance

Baheni says entire
Body throbbed with pain
But my mind experienced
Profound peace

●◞◞●

1.　　It's customarily mandatory for the Hindus to take bath after attending a funeral, before carrying out any other business.

ಬಬಬ || **38** || ಜಜಜ

Opening my eyes
When I saw forth
My eyes beheld
Pandurang

Had been to Pandhari
Kept remembering that
In front of my eyes
Was Jayram

A brahmin had then
Appeared in my dream
That memory too
Dwelt in my mind

Nothing else I saw
Before my eyes at all
Mind remembered chanting
The Lord's name

Had listened to earlier
The narratives of the Lord
My mind remembered them
Again and again

Tukoba's poems
Unparalleled renowned
Contemplating them
Mind craves

Such are whose poems
If I could meet him
Ecstatic would be
Mind mine

Engrossed with Tukoba
My mind became
Having heard his poems
During kirtan

Meeting Tukoba
Would be the occasion
Like attaining salvation
It would be for me

Opportunity to listen
To Tukoba's kirtan
Would give my mind
Contentment

Remembering Tukoba
Ever in my mind
I stayed at home
All the time

Baheni says Tuka
Is my Guru, my brother
On meeting him
Infinite

●～◆～●

ಉಉಉ || **39** || ಜಜಜ

Fish without water
As suffers endlessly
Likewise predilection
Tukoba for me

Those having gone
Through the same
Will understand it
By own experience

As the thirsty
Craves but water
Likewise entire being
Without him

Baheni says desired
For Tukoba's feet
Having listened to
His poems

● ❧ ☙ ●

ಉಉಉ || **40** || ಜಜಜ

Who can incinerate
Amassment of sins
Except the sadguru
Know this well

Therefore the need
For the supreme sadguru
Who rids of labours
Of material existence

Who else can cure
The three afflictions
Except for togetherness
With the sadguru

The cycle of birth and death
How to break away from
Without receiving blessings
From the sadguru?

Desires altogether
Will be eliminated
When Tukoba sadguru
Will meet me

Baheni says life
Seems to be fading
Why no mercy for me
O Tukoba?

ಐ ಐ ಐ ‖ **41** ‖ ಐ ಐ ಐ

Cannot utter a word
Yet mind imploring
Tukoba does not hear
What to do?

Obnoxious are past deeds
Helpful is not the Lord
Still the mind desires
What should I do?

For thirteen days
Notebooks underwater
He preserved intact
That be the truth[1]

The knowledge vedantic
In the language of Maharashtra
Spread among the masses
The all-knowing

My mind desires
Only his blessings
But he doesn't know
Of my mind

Baheni says fault
Must lie with me
He is not to be
Blamed at all

●⚭⚮●

1.	Tukaram was forced by the caste-brahmins to destroy the notebooks containing his poems by immersing them in the river Indrayani as a punishment for challenging the caste hierarchy by disseminating the vedantic knowledge despite being a non-Brahmin. The legend has it that after thirteen days, these notebooks were returned intact to Tukaram, thus preserving all his poems.

ಐಐಐ || **42** || ಖಖಖ

Great lamentation
Mind commenced
Why did you forsake me
O Vitthal?

The triad of afflictions
Torments me greatly
Why doesn't my life
End now?

Then fortuitously
On the seventh day[1]
Among reverberations
Of the Lord's praise

Before me appeared
Tukaram himself
Saying, Carry out promptly
Worldly duties

Do not worry
I am with you
Partake of the nectar
At hand

Calf approaching
Cow releases milk
Indeed it's the nectar
Partake of it

His hand upon my head
He spoke to me
Revealed the mantra
In my ear

I placed my head
On his feet earnestly
He gave me the text
Mantra Gita

It was on Sunday
Waning [2] fifth day of Kartik
In a dream I received
Blessings of Guru

Mind was filled with bliss
Immersed in the Form Supreme
Awakened, I sat up
Marvelling

Remembered the mantra
Tukoba's form

Grace absolute in the dream
That was obtained

Fed me the nectar
Of taste unequalled
Only the initiated mind
Will know of

Baheni says such
Grace of the Sadguru
Tukaram bestowed indeed
Upon me absolute

●๏๑●

1. From the death of the calf
2. Every month of the Indian lunar calendar is divided into waxing and
waning fortnights, called respectively *Shukla/Shuddha Paksh* and
Krishna/Vadya Paksha.

ఆఇఆ || **43** || ఎఞఎ

Attained contentment
By the words of the brahmin*
Remembering the poems
In my dreams

My mind perceives
But Tukoba's form
Without ever having
Beheld him

Whose poems can
Bestow such repose
His physical form must be
The same as Vitthal

Between Vitthal and him
Distinction cannot be any
This is what my mind
Firmly believes

Pandurang is Tukaram
Pandurang is Tukaram
How can they be separated
From each other?

In the Kaliyuga, the Lord
Reincarnated as the Buddha
The same has manifested
In Tukoba's form

Tukoba's intellect
The form of Pandurang
Tukoba's mind
The Form Supreme

The Driver of all
Of Tukaram's faculties
Is but Pandurang
That's the truth

Tukoba's eyes
Are but Pandurang

His ears are the Indestructible
Form Divine

Whatever is written
By Tukoba's hands
Each, each, each of it
Manifestly Pandurang

All of Tukoba's
Actions and thoughts
Lord Himself carries out
Undivided

Baheni says the Form
Omnipresent Tukoba's
In remembrance of that
My mind indulges

● ❧ ☙ ●

*For Bahinabai, a brahmin does not mean a caste-brahmin i.e. someone who
is brahmin only by their birth and not by their actions and thoughts.
Therefore, here she refers to Tukaram as the brahmin.

―――――――――――――――――――――

ಅಚಅಚಅಚ || **44** || ಜುಜುಜು

Jayram eminent
Ocean of knowledge
His mind is witness
Unto it

He had invited
Hirambhat over
To enquire after
My condition

Hirambhat told him
About everything
All that happened
In his house

Dreaming, found Guru
In Tukaram's form
She received initiation
In her dreams

On awakening
That girl sat up
She consoled the cow
Caressing it

She milked the cow
And partook it
The cow began to take
Water and fodder

However the girl is
Thoroughly transformed
Entirely enthralled
Her heart is

Engrossed in Tukoba
Her mind has become

Her mother and father
Dissuade her

Her husband seems
To have gone insane
He just sits staring
In her direction

Being obsessed
She sits at home
Directing her mind
On Tukoba

Such happenings
Hirambhat reported
Jayram in his mind
Was delighted

Baheni says having
Heard all this
Jayram Swami
Blessed me

●ಞಞ●

ಞಞಞ || **45** || ಜಜಜ

Jayram Swami
Bestowed his grace
Came to perceive
My condition

On seeing him
I was delighted
Choked on words
Overjoyed

I made offering of lamps
Folded hands, in my mind
Worshipped him elaborately
In my mind

Baheni says intent
Of my mind
Recognised certainly
Pandurang

● ৶ৡ ●

ಞಞಞ || **46** || ಜಜಜ

A glance of grace
He cast upon me
Like that of a mother
Affectionate

Accepted mine
Worship implicit
Then the kindhearted
Left for home

There he sat down
For meditation unbidden

Drawing inwards
All faculties

Then what occurred
Was unprecedented
Tukaram appeared
Before him

Folded hands devoutly
Embraced joyfully
My master, my benefactor
Became ecstatic

Also appeared before me
Although momentarily
He put a morsel
In my mouth

Then he told me,
I came to meet Jayram
Also recognized
Your mind

You all must not
Stay here anymore
Path of the Knowledge Supreme
Do not shun

Baheni says Tukoba
Appeared before me
For the second time
Via mind's faculties

ಅಅಅ || **47** || ಜಜಜ

Such was amazement
Of the people around
They would rush in
To see me

On seeing them
Husband of mine
Would inflict pain
Upon my body

He couldn't bear it
Detested the people
His detestation increased
Moment by moment

Saying, it's better
If this woman dies
Why do these folks
Pay her visits?

Whether she has been
Possessed by some spirit?
How is God going to
Provide for her?

Baheni says such were
My husband's worries
On knowing the Lord Infinite
I came to know

●⊷ఇ●

ಆಆಆ || **48** || ಜುಜುಜು

My husband would say,
We are the brahmins
We recite the Vedas
All the while

Who's Tuka but a shudra
Due to his dream-appearances
My wife is corrupted
What should I do?

Who is Jayram?
Who is Pandurang?
My married life lies
In utter ruins

Whatever do we know
Of chanting God's name
Never even dreamt
Of devotion

What of the good and the godly?
What's all about devotion?
To the ranks of alms-receivers
We forever belong

Baheni says such
Thoughts flooded his mind
My husband made a resolve
Unwavering

●༄༅●

ఆఆఆ || **49** || ಐಐಐ

My husband had made
A resolve in his mind,
I should take to wilderness
Forsaking her now

People would soon
Be touching her feet
She wouldn't give a fig
About me then

They would come to her
To understand scriptures
She would take me then
For a lowly borne

People come to our home
Asking for her already
As if I, the brahmin,
Am a moron

They've begun to call her
The godly woman
Who is going to suffer me
In front of her?

Baheni says thus
Went on in his mind
Immersed in these thoughts
He reassured himself

●❧❦●

ಆಓಓಓ || **50** || ಖಖಖ

He'd say, O mind,
The state of the woman!
You most certainly
Must not stay

Start instantly, let's go
On pilgrimage, detached
What a misfortune
Has befallen us?

He bowed down
To parents-in-law,
This woman is pregnant
Of three months

I am leaving now
On a pilgrimage
Let the godly woman
Carry on

I will never see
Her face again
How will I get out
Of this disgrace?

Who will stay here
Bear this humiliation?
Who will provide for
Such a woman?

Baheni says thus
Spoke my husband
To the consternation
Of my mind

●❧❧●

ॐॐॐ || **51** || ॐॐॐ

What can be done
To what is predestined?
One has to undergo
What one must

I am not taken
Over by spirits
Possessed is not
Body mine

Performing my duties
With all my heart
I will appease the gods
Adhering to precepts

Service to my husband
He is my only god
My husband is for me
The Being Supreme

Water from his feet
Be all the holy waters

Without that water
Rest is futile

If I ever transgress
My husband's biddings
On my head be all the sins
Of this earth

All the four goals[1]
Of life are to be attained
With the husband alone
The Vedas decree

This is my resolve
Desire of my mind
All faculties directed
To my husband

By serving my husband
I'll attain the Goal Supreme
In my husband rests all
My self-interest

Except my husband
My mind remembers
If any other gods
That be the sin ultimate

My husband is the sadguru
My husband is all the means
This is the firm belief
Of my mind

Baheni says, o Lord
You entered
My husband's mind
Calmed him

● ❧ ❧ ●

1.   *Dharma* (धर्म) – righteousness, moral goals
    Artha (अर्थ) – prosperity, financial goals
Kam (काम) – pleasure, love, psychological goals
Moksha (मोक्ष) – salvation, spiritual goals

ଓଓଓ ‖ **52** ‖ ଓଓଓ

If husband goes away
Taking up detachment*
What do I live for
O Pandurang?

Body without life
How can be adorned?
What is the moonshine
Without night?

My husband is life
And I am the body
My husband is all the good
That happened to me

My husband is water
I am the fish within

How can I survive
Without him?

My husband is the sun
I am his irradiance
How is it possible to be
Separated from him?

Baheni says this
Resolve of my mind
Expressing my thoughts
The Lord knows

● ❧ ❧ ●

Vairagya (वैराग्य) - the mental state and resultant act of renouncing worldly pleasures and pursuits by taking up a solitary stay in the wilderness to undertake sustained meditation in order to attain salvation

───────────────────

ෞෞෞ ‖ **53** ‖ ෞෞෞ

Upon husband's
Taking up detachment
I will end my life
Decidedly

My body laid lifeless
For the sake of the calf
He is but essentially
The Being Supreme

Without receiving
Water from husband's feet
All the food that I eat
Be meat for me*

If I do not receive
My husband's leftovers
Upon my head be the sins
Of all the three worlds

If my mind wanders
Away from my husband
How could I wish at all
To remain alive?

Even if one day goes by
Without seeing my husband
Piling upon of great sins
That would be

Baheni says for me
The precept is sacrosanct
For me my husband is
The Being Eternal

*Eating meat is forbidden for the brahmin sand is considered to be one of the greatest sins one can commit. Such was the severity of this taboo, that even touching the meat accidentally would render the person an outcaste instantaneously.

ಚಚಚ || **54** || ಋಋಋ

Vitthal is of rocks
Tuka is of dreams
Why should I keep
From the real bliss?

I will partake infinite
This bliss in service
This is what the Vedas too
Expect of me

The dutiful wife
Who serves her husband
She does attain salvation
For both the clans

Baheni says solace
Of my being
My husband is the end
Of births and deaths

● ❧ ☙ ●

ಚಚಚ || **55** || ಋಋಋ

My husband had
Resolved in his mind
To depart, forsaking me
In a day or two

Then an illness
Inflicted his body
Suffered inflammation
For seven days

He would not listen
To our acquaintances
I remained by his side
Day and night

He would not take
Any medication we gave
Anguish excruciating
He endured

For an entire month
He could not eat
Anguish extraordinary
He endured

Committed pledges
To great many gods
Prayers for deliverance
Offered distinct

But his sufferings
Saw no ebbing
He'd say, Death
Has come for me

Is it for denouncing
Pandurang and Tukoba

That these afflictions
Have stricken me?

If I am suffering
From all these maladies
Owing to denouncing
Tukaram

Then forgive me now
Bestow grace upon me
O universally revered
Tukaram

Baheni says my husband
Was filled with remorse
Pandurang everything
Witnesses

●❧❧●

ॐॐॐ || **56** || ॐॐॐ

Then arrived an elderly brahmin
He asked my husband,
Why do you desire
To be dead?

Why has your mind
Become so detached?
Have you forsaken your wife
For what reason?

You first should introspect
Whether she is at fault
Then perhaps express
Your wrath

If you wish at all
To save your life
You must accept her
Wholeheartedly

If she ever fails
To perform her duties
Then do forsake her
You silly man

She is a detached
Determined devotee
You should be the same
Most certainly

Then all will be well
Thus he spoke
My husband fell
Upon his feet

My husband explained
Everything to him,
Pray bestow upon me
Boon of life

Please save me, o master
From this affliction

I will devote my life
At your feet

I will not say a word
To my wife ever again
I will surrender earnestly
Before the Lord

Rose up, reverently
Folded his hands
Then all will be well
Said the brahmin

I too was listening
To their conversation
At my husband's feet
I prostrated

That brahmin disappeared
Instantaneously then
My husband's health
Was restored

Baheni says when the Lord
Showers his blessings
Everything that one desires
Arrives at the doorstep

● ❧ ☙ ●

ಚಾಚಾಚ || **57** || ಜುಜುಜು

My husband regained
His health soon
His affliction diminished
Day by day

He softened towards me
With contentment he spoke
All his detestation earlier
Having dissipated

Now we all must
Leave from here
We ought to return
To our place

The Lord himself appeared
Before us as the brahmin
He has delineated well
Our future

We must follow his words
Devoting to the Lord's service
I have stopped bothering
About the inheritance

Both my parents
He tried to persuade,
Please return to Devgaon
Unworried

We both will settle down
Somewhere in the forest
Remembering the name
Of the Lord

Whether all be well
Or be it otherwise
We'll undertake in entirety
Service to the Lord

We will take residence
In Tukoba's village
With all the determination
Of the mind

Such a transformation
My husband underwent
My Lord Gracious witnesses
Everything

Whatever is not possible
For the Lord to make happen?
Indeed this be the experience
Of the masses

Baheni say then
We all departed
Arriving at Dehu*
To behold Tukoba

●❧☙●

*Tukaram's native place, approx. 30 km to the north of Pune

ಞಞಞ || **58** || ಬಙಬ

The mother of the calf
The black cow was with us
She would run enrapt
Ahead of us

Along with parents
Brother and husband
Arrived on the banks
Of the Indrayani

After taking holy dip
Went to Pandurang temple
My entire being was
Filled with bliss

Tukoba was performing
The ceremony of lamps there
I joined my hands reverently
Keeping calm

He looked exactly the same
As seen in my dreams
I humbly gazed at him
Wholesightedly

Baheni says my husband
Prostrated at his feet there
With all the devotion
Of his heart

● App●

ಅಅಅ || **59** || ಬಬಬ

Today my life has become fruitful, o beloved
Having beholden the feet of the good and the godly
Dust from their feet relieves body's burden
Such bliss is bestowed infinite

Today great fortune has shone upon me
Beheld the feet of the good and the godly
Mighty love has taken over my being
Bliss itself blissed out readily

Constricted I was in one, now became many
If observed, I am expanded all over the universe
Like the mighty oak springs out of an acorn
I myself have become everything

Regained lost consciousness, delusion shattered
Till now I was acting under the grand illusion
Mendacious delusion of the rope being the snake
Shattered on beholding dust from his feet

Baheni says he has undone my self-absorption
Relieved me of the afflictions of material existence
On meeting Tukaram, my life became meaningful
I have attained the ultimate

ॐॐॐ || **60** || ॐॐॐ

Noontime was nigh
And food was required
My Husband roamed through
The entire village

At that time there was
A brahmin named Kondaji
He said, Pray come to my place
To have a meal

My husband replied,
We are five people
How can anybody
Feed so many?

He said to my husband,
Do not worry, o master
You all are invited
For the meal

Go and find a place
For your stay now
Do come to my home
At noontime

Baheni says my husband
Returned and told us
That he had arranged
For food

●⸱❧⸱●

ಞಞಞ || **61** || ಋಋಋ

Mambaji Gosavi
Was a resident there
His expansive house
We had seen

We went to him
Requested for shelter
But he was capricious
Short-tempered

He charged at us
And drove us out
We besought shelter
At Anand Owari*

Settling down there
We went to have meal
A pleasant experience
At Kondaji's

He enquired after us,
Where have you come from?
Why have you undertaken
This journey?

We told him everything
What had happened earlier
He said, Pray be our guests
On this occasion

On coming Monday
Happens to be new moon
Stay here and partake joy
Of devotion

Continual kirtan be
There at the temple
Tukoba is mother dear
To all the Vaishnavas

Do stay here you all
Have your meals with us
It is great fortune for us
To have you all

Baheni says thence
We all stayed at Dehu
With absolute devotion
Towards Tukoba

*Tukaram's ancestral house at Dehu has a Vitthal temple in it. This temple
had a spacious verandah outside, where Tukaram would sit composing his
poems and also would perform kirtans there. It is on this verandah that
Bahinabai's family took shelter on their arrival at Dehu.

ఆఆఆ || **62** || ಜಜಜ

Kirtan in the temple
Would be all the while
I would listen to devoutly
Day and night

Tukoba's kirtan
Interpretation of the Vedas
My mind would obtain
Contentment

Tukoba's physical form
I had seen previously
In my dreams
At Kolhapur

Seeing with my eyes
The same form for real
My eyes would well up
With great joy

Be it the day or night
I could not sleep at all
Tukoba had taken over
My mind

Baheni says I would
Sway with ecstasy
Those with the experience
Will understand

ಜಜಜ || **63** || ಜಜಜ

Mambaji Gosavi
Said to my husband,
Become my disciple
Along with your wife

This is my desire
You, too, are devout
Both of you look
So detached

Listening to the same
On occasions many
Then he told him
Deferentially,

We have been initiated
Already previously
He would not believe
Any of it

My husband told him
Everything of the past
What happened earlier
At Kolhapur

On listening to that
He was filled with hatred
Saying, What satisfaction
In dreams?

Until service to Guru
Has not been rendered
Until the Sadguru has not
Placed hand on head

How can that Guru
Be considered real?
How can a shudra* ever
Be knowledgeable?

Initiation in dreams
A shudra as Guru
That too a peasant
Utterly ignorant

I will get you banished
From the ranks of the brahmins
Don't you dare to talk to me
Of devotion to Guru

Baheni says thus
Mambaji denounced
Began to persecute us
From that moment

*Tukaram was born in a so-called lower caste viz. kunabi (कुणबी), as such the caste brahmins considered him incapable of and ineligible for receiving/imparting spiritual knowledge.

ಆಞಞಞ || **64** || ಞಞಞಞ

One day on the way
I came across Mambaji
He seemed to be entirely
Hell-bent

I showed him respect
Trying to touch his feet
He did not allow me
Running away

Then he said to me,
I don't know your caste
So I will consider you
As shudras

Are you of goldsmiths
Or *golak** by caste
You have no privileges
Of the brahmins

If you ever go to have food
Anywhere as such a privilege
I will drag you all then
To the court of law

Baheni says things
Having heard these
I told my husband
All of them

●❦❦●

*A sub-caste among the brahmins which is considered to be of inferior
lineage

____

ಆಬಆಬ || **65** || ಬಬಬ

Mahadaji Kulkarni*
Told these things
To Kondaji Pant
All that happened

Then he took us all
In his own house
Saying, Mambaji has
No other work

But he continued
Persecuting us increasingly
Plotting and scheming
Trying to kill us

Saying, Brahmins these
But their Guru shudra
This is what he kept
Harping on

This persecution reached
Such an extreme extent
All the people around
Came to know

Baheni says the Lord
Torments in so many ways
In order to test
My resolve

● ❧ ❧ ●

*The revenue collector of Dehu village, and a devout follower of Tukaram

---

ಖಖಖ || **66** || ಋಋಋ

My devotion is not superficial
My mind is welded to Your feet

Ready to face what may come
I surrender to You alone, my Lord

Cares I give none for material existence
For I have embraced Your feet

Foes would torment and persecute
But these Your feet in my mind

Even if they pierce fingernails with needles
I will not let go of You, dear Lord

For You are the only Saviour
Baheni says have mercy on me

● ❧ ❧ ●

ಞಞಞ || **67** || ಜಜಜ

Apaji Gosavi[1]
Resided at Pune
A renowned *rajayogi*[2]
He was

A letter addressing him
Mambaji had dispatched,
Tukoba, the god-man
Is a shudra, a grocer

He performs kirtan
In the temple all the time
Even the brahmins fall
At his feet

Rameshwar Bhat[3] is
Extremely distinguished
He too bows down to him
Reverentially

I find all these things
Exceedingly offensive
For all this is wrongful
Against the Vedas

You are the right authority
To punish such an offence
Putting him in shackles
Take in your custody

Apart from him, there is
One husband and wife
They too call themselves
His disciples

They claim to be brahmins
Although of the goldsmiths
Even Kulkarni[4] has greatly
Esteemed them

Grievous threat I perceive
To true religion in all this
Therefore I am sending
This dispatch

If chastisement is not
Rendered unto him
The State too will go
To the dogs

Quackery pretentious
Threatens true religion
It must be protected
O chief of lords

Baheni says such
Letter he had sent
Written clandestinely
In his house

● ❧ ☙ ●

1.	Apaji Gosavi (आपाजी गोसावी) - The highest administrative official of the then Pune province

2.	Rajayogi (राजयोगी) - A statesman of highest spiritual calibre who performs his worldly duties without being attached to material existence.

3.	Rameshwar Bhat (रामेश्वर भट) - One of the erstwhile brahmin persecutors of Tukaram, who later became one of his most ardent followers, the writer of the most recited eulogy to Tukaram

4.	Mahadaji Kulkarni (महादजी कुलकर्णी) had given shelter as well as protection to Bahinabai's family during their stay at Dehu to Mambaji's utter consternation.

ೞೞೞ || **68** || ೞೞೞ

Apaji Gosavi
Read the letter
It infuriated him
Tremendously,

Despite being shudra
He allows touching feet
What a horrific sin
He commits

Despite being goldsmith
They call themselves brahmin
One must not even see
Their faces

Brahmins are becoming
Disciples of a shudra

This is the transgression
Paramount

They must be punished
He is not alone to be blamed
Thus he ascertained
Decidedly

Baheni says he wrote
A reply to Mambaji,
Befitting action will be
Duly taken

●◦ℳ◦●

ಙಙಙ || **69** || ಜಜಜ

Mambaji's heart was
Filled with hatred
Saying, You must leave
This place

It would keep my mind
Occupied with worries
Why this hindrance
In my devotion?

Never stole from anyone
Never badmouthed anyone
Nor are we wrongdoers
Why this hatred then?

I would implore the Lord
Keeping Him ever in mind
You are my only witness
O Pandurang

Whatever in my mind
Is known to You alone
Not even traces of hatred
In my heart

This hindrance You brought up
You ought to eliminate it
You have been testing
Tukoba too

You always keep tormenting
Those who worship You
Devotion through tests many
You assess

Baheni says o Lord
Predestined are
All joys and sorrows
That befall

● ❧ ❧ ●

ಚಚಚ || **70** || ಜಜಜ

The cow from Kolhapur
Was still with us there
That cow would still
Give milk

Mambaji tied that cow
Locked up inside his house
He thrashed her up
With a thick stick

We searched for the cow
Couldn't find her anywhere
Tukoba suffered great deal
At that time

He saw in his dream
The cow in distress
Tied up to a pole
For three nights

No fodder or water
She yelped in pain
No way to escape
Could find

When Tukoba woke up
He found his back
Too badly swollen up
To be cured

Bruises were seen
On Tukoba's back
He urged Vithoba
Every which way

Seeing his sufferings
People were distressed
All about his dream
He told them

Then Tukoba invoked
The Lord in his mind,
For my deliverance
Rush o Lord

Unable to know where
Who has tied the cow
Pray rush, o my Lord
Protect the cow

Then all of a sudden
Mambaji's house
Burst into flames
Weltering

People ran for help
Extinguished the fire
The cow trapped inside
Was bellowing,

Searched for the cow
For last three days

This despicable man
Had tied her up

They rescued the cow
Brought her outside
They found the cow
Beaten on the back

They immediately sent
For my husband,
Take good care
Of his cow, o brahmin

Tukoba rushed there
Circumambulated the cow,
I salute your virtues
You are great indeed

You had appeared
In my dream, o mother
I knew not where to find you
Then I urged the Lord

Yours and mine
Is but one soul pervasive
That I am convinced of
Entirely now

When such intense words
Tukoba spoke there
My mind experienced
Great anguish

I too underwent
The same agony
Vitthal is witness
All-knowing

People would see
Tukoba's back
Seeing the cow
They'd get distressed

Baheni says thus
It transpired then
Tribulations of the cow
The Lord knows

●⋙⋘●

ಐಐಐ || **71** || ಬಬಬ

Rameshwar Bhatt
Having heard the news
Arrived thereupon
With great hurry

He too met Tukoba
With folded hands
Minutely examined
The cow as well

Both of their backs
Looked so identical

All the people there
Couldn't hold tears

Who can fathom
Tukoba's eminence
Of this Kaliyug
He is Pralhad*

Calling upon all
He extolled his virtues
Everyone immersed
In ecstasy

Baheni says all
People proclaimed,
Tukoba manifestly
Pandurang

● ৰু৬৵ ●

---

*Pralhad (प्रल्हाद) - One of the greatest devotees of Lord Vishnu, renowned for his unshakable devotion despite the incessant misfortunes befalling him.

ಐಐಐ || **72** || ಜಜಜ

Mahadaji Kulkarni
Had sheltered us
We stayed there long
Unfazed

Blows of sorrows
Befell great many
The Lord alone
Knows it all

Faced all hardships
With faith in the Lord
Stayed unshakeable
Steadfastly

Then in due time
I gave birth
A daughter was
Born to me

She was named
As Kashibai
All the rites were
Duly performed

Baheni says the calf
That died at Kolhapur
Seemed to be reborn
As my daughter

● ∽ᴥᴖ● ●

ఇఱఱఱ || **73** || ಜಱಱ

Sins amassed exhausted
Mind too got cleansed
The longing of the heart
Recognized

Blessed by the Lord
The banks of Indrayani
Heritage of devotion
In Dehu village

There is the temple
Of Lord Pandurang
A place to reside
Found there

Tukaram, the saints
Performed kirtan there
Dawn to dusk, these three
Stayed before my eyes

Afraid of my husband
I couldn't serve him
But my mind stayed
Ever at his feet

Baheni says thus
Passed months seven
All sins amassed seem
To have depleted

● ❧ ☙ ●

‖ **74** ‖

The verandah of the temple
Was called Anand Owari
I yearned for long
To sit there

In deep meditation
With eyes half-opened
Immersed in remembering
Lord Vithoba

Then all of a sudden
While I was left staring
Tukaram arrived there
In the form of Guru

Baheni says thereafter
With mother's consent
I spent three nights
At Anand Owari

‖ **75** ‖

Knew no meditation
Knew no liturgy
How to form posture
I knew not

What is the key to focus?
How to restrain senses?
I had never received
Any instruction

Knew only Vithoba's form
Carved into stone
My heart's indulgence
Lord's praise

To perform kirtan
In front of Tukoba
That was the longing
Of my mind

When got to listen to
*Taal-chiplya** resonating
My heart could not
Contain my joy

With eyes half-opened
Awakening in slumber
I beheld Tukoba
In front of me

He spoke to me
Placed hand on my head
He bestowed upon me
The boon of poetry

Baheni says knew not
Dreaming or awakened
Ceased to function
All my senses

● ⚘⚘ ●

*Chiplya (चिपळ्या) - Percussion (struck idiophones) instrument used by the
Varkaris while performing bhajan and kirtan

---

୫୫୫ || **76** || ୱୱୱ

Joy overwhelmed
All of my senses
Tukaram's feet
Remembered

Regained consciousness
Opened my eyes
Remembered the mantra
Hexasyllabic

Imprinted on memory
Deep in my mind
Anything else at all
Remembered not

Baheni says his hand
He placed on my head
The body in this world
Didn't seem to exist

ಆಆಆ || **77** || ಜಜಜ

Describing that Bliss
Silences the speech
Known to the fortunate
Those devoted to Guru

Joy is experienced
By all my senses too
Having seated beside
The Energy Absolute

Like a pot submerged
Into deep water
Fills through and through
Without breaking

Baheni says likewise
Happened to my mind
Tukaram recognises
All those signs

● ∾ ∾ ●

ಆಆಆ || **78** || ಜಜಜ

I felt I shouldn't get up
Even at the cost of life
Such was the Bliss
Saturating my heart

With unfettered mind
Overfilled with joy
I went to the Indrayani
Took a holy dip

I went to the temple
To behold Panduranga
Inspiration visited upon me
To compose poems

I paid reverence
To Tukoba there
Returning home
Immediately

Baheni says my mind
Began to compose
Like the sea advances
With the moon in the sky

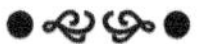

ABHANG AT NIRYAN

The autobiographical poems that Bahinabai wrote after the previous one till the ones written five days before her death have unfortunately gone missing. None of the efforts in the first half as well as the second of the twentieth century have succeeded in discovering any manuscripts containing poems pertaining to Bahinabai's life from her age of 19 to 72 years! Almost 50 years of Bahinabai's life have been entirely wiped out. What makes this loss infinitely unfortunate is the fact that these are the poems that would be speaking about Tukaram's final days. Had these poems been available today, we would have got a first-hand account of what exactly transpired in Dehu during those fateful years!

***

Bahinabai's poems that follow are labelled as *niryanache* (निर्याणाचे) or *niryanpar* (निर्याणपर) abhang i.e. abhang composed at the time of departure. Bahinabai had composed these autobiographical abhang in her final five days and they are addressed to her son, Vitthal whose replies, too, can be found in Bahinabai's Gatha. However, his replies are not included in this translation.

ಐಐಐ || **79** || ಜುಜುಜು

Farewell to Rukmini
We have bidden
I too have to tread
The same path

Hence decided to send
Letter instantly to Godavari[1]
Lest you be robbed
Off the duties of a son

Leave everything
Chores or business
Threshold of Death
Awaits me

Therefore I wrote
The letter promptly
The flag of Death
Stands ahead

Give food to the brahmins
On the thirteenth day[3]
Leave, having that done
Expeditiously

Five days from now
Be the end of my life
With bated breath
I am waiting

The very first day
Of the month of *Ashvin*[4]
Threshold of Death
Is destined

Baheni says for you
The duties of a son await
Therefore rush forth
At the earliest

1.	These poems composed over the last five days of her life by Bahinabai are in the form of a dialogue between her son Vitthal and herself. Apparently, she composed and dictated these poems - while literally counting her final moments - and Vitthal wrote them down.
2.	Vitthal was away from home to perform the final rites of his wife, Rukmini on the banks of the river Godavari and therefore the need for this letter.
3.	On the thirteenth day from the death (तेरावे), ceremonial food is offered to the brahmins as part of the final rites.
4.	Ashvin (अश्विन) - Seventh month of the Indian lunar calendar, coinciding with the month of October of the Gregorian calendar

---

೮೮೮ || **80** || ೞೞೞ

Receiving the letter
You arrived promptly
Making great haste
My dear son

Performed final rites
Rukmini's thirteenth day

With such a heavy heart
Speech falters

An ideal husband
An ideal son too
Devoted mind, body
In entirety

Seeing you returned
I felt such contentment
Overwhelming affection
Faltered my speech

On the very first day
Of the month of Ashvin
Be the end of my life
Know this well

Let not any sorrows
Find place in your heart
Do not transgress
These my biddings

You have performed well
All the duties of a son
You have arrived promptly
At my final moments

Baheni says now, child
Ask what you will
Let not there be any
Qualms in your heart

ಬಚಬಚ || **81** || ಬಬಬ

I have listened earnestly
To what you just spoke
Whatever that you have
Decided so far

I appreciate greatly
The place you chose*
But do listen to first
What I have to say

There's not much time
To reach that place
Moment of my death is
Approaching fast

First day of the next month
I intend to shed this body
And today happens to be
Third last day of this month

That's why I tell you
What I have resolved
For me the holiest water
Is the *Pranita* of Shivpur

Even Ravan had performed
His legendary worship here
He had successfully propitiated
Lord Shankar here

Here Ravan had offered
His nine heads to the Lord
Eighty eight thousand rishis
Were present there

Gods including Bramhadev
Participated in the yajna
Such eminent be holy waters
Of this Shivpur

Bathing after the yajna
They blessed this place,
All the holy waters be
Present here

There is no holy waters
To match the *Pranita*
On this entire earth,
Proclaimed Lord Shankar,

Kashi, Gaya, all holy waters
Converge in this place
Remembering this, you all
Take a holy dip

Therefore in my mind
This is what I have resolved
My heart is convinced
Of it entirely

Uphold my words these
With utmost reverence

And be at peace
With yourself

Baheni says, o son
I told you my mind
To carry it out
Be prepared

●⤳⤶●

*Vitthal, Bahinabai's son, intended to take her to the banks of the holy
Godavari for her final moments and he had done the necessary
arrangements before returning home.

ಅಞಞ ॥ **82** ॥ ಚುಚುಚು

Holy waters, pilgrimages
Performed bounden duties
Thus underwent twelve births
Both, you and me

You have been borne
My son for the thirteenth time
You do not remember
Of course, any of it

For thirteen births
We have been together
Unprecedented unimpaired
Steadfastly

In conceiving you
I was blessed too
Such is the bond
I speak of, dear son

Unflinching dedication
To husband is my religion
I would not delve further
Lest this tome swells up

I wish to listen now
To entire *Dnyaneshwari**
For I am left with
A few moments

Baheni says henceforth
I would not be reborn
I am thoroughly rid of
All desires

●❧ॐ●

Dnyaneshwari (ज्ञानेश्वरी) - The founding – and the most revered – text of the
Varkari sect written by Sant Dnyandev in 1290 CE

―――――――――――――――――――――――

ఠఠఠ || **83** || ಜಜಜ

Godavari, Bhagirathi
Yamuna, Sarasvati
Tapi, Bhogavati
All holy waters

Will arrive in the Pranita
At the time of my demise
Keep your mind calm
My dear son

Krishna, Tungbhadra
Bhima, Phalgu, Reva
Pushkar, too, all holy waters
Of this earth

All the deities, too,
Will arrive at that time
You will be witnessing
Death at its grandest

When along with rishis all
Pandurang will stand
At the time of my death
Surrounding me

Baheni says falsehoods
You might think these be
I will unravel the truth
For you now

●~❧☙~●

ಬಬಬ || **84** || ಬಬಬ

What holy waters can equal
The Knowledge Supreme?
The enlightened ones know this
On the merit of pious acts

Wherein the mind
Is cleansed of impurities
Holy water this acclaimed
By all the scriptures

In order to bathe in it
Went by twelve births
To cleanse the impurities
Of the mind

In this thirteenth birth
Received the means
Bathing wherein
No rebirth

I was striving in vain
Practising other means
Since I had deviated
From the right path

Here desires unwholesome
Are cleansed of impurities
This be the true holy waters
For the enlightened ones

Whose all urges are extinct
That mind is enlightened one
That be the holy waters
The most exalted

Do contemplate upon
What I have told you
For extrinsic holy waters
I have no desire

Baheni says all urges
Submerged within the One
That is the true definition
Of holy waters

ಞಞಞ || **85** || ಜಜಜಜ

At my final moments
Sky will be cloudless
All directions you will see
Radiant white

Let this be imbibed
Upon your heart
Stay firm on what
I bade you

Gods would set off
Arriving in aircrafts here

Know that ebullitions three
Will be felt

Son, you will find me
Inside your heart
Having been cremated
Physically evanesced

Baheni says do have
Faith in my words
Tukaram be witness
To all of this*

● ☙ ❧ ●

*In the abhang that follow, Bahinabai has recounted 12 of her previous
births. These abhang can be found in the Kolhatkar Text, abhang 91-98.
These abhang are not included in this translation, as they have no bearing on
the present autobiography.

ॐॐॐ || **86** || ॐॐॐ

Seventy-two years[1]
Expanse of this life
Today attained it[2]
Lotus-seated

Now my final moments
Are fast approaching
That's why narrated
All thirteen births

Sixteen *prahar*[3] more
Are remaining now
Prepare your mind
Dear son

Time of my death
The fifth should be
Confirm it with yourself
At the moment of my death

Baheni says thirteen
Births narrated all
Able to narrate a bit
Guru's blessings

1. This is stanza 38 of abhang 99 from the Kolhatkar Text. Stanzas 1-37
recount Bahinabai's autobiography, hence they are not included here to
avoid repetition.
2. This mention of her birthday makes this abhang crucial
for determining Bahinabai's timeline.
3. Prahar (प्रहर) - Ancient Indian unit of measuring time, 1 *prahar* = 3 hours

---

ಚಚಚ || **87** || ಚುಚುಚು

Thirteen births today
I have narrated to you
Being visible to me
Each of them

Knowing today
To be the apt time
Narrated all to you
In the final hours

Eighteen days ago
I came to know my death
But didn't share with you
I will tell you why

After Rukmini's death
You were meant to go
To the banks of the Godavari
To perform her final rites

She passed away
Eighteen days ago
Rukmini was indeed
An ideal wife

You would be grieved
If told about my death then
You wouldn't have gone
To Godavari for the rites

Therefore I didn't tell
About my demise
Thinking of what
Would happen

After you had left
I told all the people

Whatever that was
In my heart,

Rukmini's final rites
Once get performed
You should dispatch
The letter

Five days remaining
To my death
When I told this
To the people

Then I got written down
All the verses I remembered
Do rewrite them afterwards
Remove errors

Baheni says the Lord
Makes me compose
Those who don't believe
May go to hell

●ల౪●

ಅಅಅ || **88** || ಜಜಜ

At the time of death
One ought to be alert
Being conscious steadfastly
Of the Supreme Being

Thus spake the Lord
In the Bhagavad Gita
Today is that end
For me

The Might of the Sacred Fire
Is in my body today
The Eternal Flame radiates
Within my heart

The day of my death occurs
In the fortnight of waxing moon
This much I have already
Got confirmed

It's true that today doesn't
Happen to be *uttarayan**
But being Sadguru's decision
It matters not

I will be seated
Facing the North
Mustering courage
I'll inhibit breath

On remembering Sadguru
All five yogas
Have come to fruition
In entirety for me

Baheni says the key
Is revealed to you
What lies ahead
I will tell you

● ⚬⚬ ●

*Uttarayan (उत्तरायण) - Period between Makara Sankranti (which occurs around 14th January) and Karka Sankranti (which occurs around 16th July), considered to be auspicious

---

൫൫൫ || **89** || ೞೞೞ

Facing the North
I shall be seated
In a simple position
At my final hour

Three *ghatikas*[1]
Before the sunrise
I shall be seated
In deep meditation

At that time, dear son
Be seated behind me
Mind focused steadfastly
On the Supreme Being

External sounds varied
Will fall on your ears

Keep the Lord in your heart
At that time

Let the Lord's praise
Reverberate everywhere
For it be a grand day
Of great rejoicing

Remember the spot
That I will touch then
Know in your mind
There be the life spirit

Three and thirteen
For sixteen *ghatikas*
I will be seated
In deep meditation

Nine *ghatikas* incessant
Chanting of Lord's name
I tell you the resolve
Of my heart

Seven *ghatikas* next
Distributed thus
All the senses be brought
To a standstill

Four *ghatikas* in meditation
I will be seated still
You should keep calm
At that time

Thus will pass by
Thirteen *ghatikas*
I will chant then
My Guru's name

Chanting Tukaram
Remembering Gangadhar
Memory of the lineage
Of my Guru-lineage[2]

Afterwards focus
On the tip of the nose
Closing the fists
Of both hands

Then I will myself
Wear basil garlands
You should be prepared
At your heart

Concentrating all
Breaths into cessation[3]
Preparing all the way
For the final breath

Steadfast in heart
The Form of the Lord
Mind will stay immersed
At that time

Perpetual indivisible
Heart-encompassing

Remembering only
The Indivisible

Baheni says such
Be my final hours
Told of the end
With resolve

●⚬⚬●

1. One *ghatika* = 24 minutes
2. Bahinabai's Guru-lineage: Adinath > Machchhindranath >
    Gorakshanath > Nivruttinath > Dnyandev > Sachchidanand >
    Vishwambhar > Raghav Chaitanya > Keshav Chaitanya >
    Babaji Chaitanya > Tukaram > Bahinabai
    (Abhang 1, *Kolhatkar Text*)
3. A Yogic practice of highest order

With the blessings of the Saints
The edifice attained fruition

Dnyandev laid the foundations
Erected the pantheon

Namdev its champion
He constructed the precinct

Janardan Ekanath
Provided pillar of *Bhagavata*

Tuka has become its spire
Sing His praise unrushed

Baheni the flag atop
Has chronicled admiringly

Appendix I

VAJRASUCHI UPANISHAD
(वज्रसूची उपनिषद)

Vajrasuchi Upanishad is one of the very first unequivocal attacks on caste-hegemony of the brahmins. It is a systematic rebuttal of the caste-brahminical claim that it is the Vedas who have bestowed supremacy on them by birth. Bahinabai, having met in person the very personification of the brahmin as defined by this text, in the form of Tukaram, was naturally drawn to it and undertook its translation. Sanskrit text of the *Vajrasuchi Upanishad* can be found here:
www.sitarammmhatre.foundation/vajrasuchi

1.

Among the four Varnas
The brahmins are superior
In whose company
The Salvation be

The brahmin is the Supreme Being,
Thus proclaim the Vedas
The dictum is revered
In the worlds three

No damnation ever
On becoming the brahmin
All the gods worship
The brahmin

Baheni says whose
Body is but the abode
For the *Gayatri**
To dwell in

●❧☙●

*One of the most revered mantras from the *Rigveda*, composed by Sage
Vishvamitra and dedicated to the Sun god, its personification in the form of
a goddess

2.

Who is to be called
The brahmin definitively?
This needs to be determined
Rationally

Then they be revered
Worshipped with great love
Givers of salvation decidedly,
Says the Veda

Being, body, caste
Complexions, deeds, duties
Which one of these
Be the key?

Baheni says whether
Knowledge and erudition
Make a Brahmin
Needs to be ascertained first

●⬿ ⬿●

3.

Being is the brahmin
If we assume thus now
It does not make
Much sense

The birds and the beasts
Creatures most heinous
The same being is found
In all of them

There will be beings
There had been many
They did not attain
Brahminness

Baheni says the Being
One in all creatures
Brahminness cannot be
Ascertained thereby

●❧☙●

4.

Body is the brahmin
If we assume thus now
It will not stand the scrutiny
Of reason

Determine conscientiously
Who be the brahmin first
Then in their worship
You will find bliss

Body is the same for all
Know this well

Presence of five elements
In every being

Youth and senescence
Childhood to the body
That be the abode
Of the being

Being for the body
Body for the being
How can they be
Called brahmin?

Baheni says the bodies
Of all the species
Are to be found the same
When scrutinised

5.

Dotage, death, fear
Same for all people
How to call them
The brahmin then?

Therefore necessary
To understand rationally
The significance of the term
The brahmin

Cremating the bodies
Of mother and father
Why doesn't it make one
Brahmin-killer?

Baheni says the body
Makes not the brahmin
When one examines it
Rationally

●⤳⤲●

6.

Now if we determine
Complexion makes the brahmin
Our experience does not
Correspond with it

When we examine carefully
Brahminness appears
Definitely to be distinct
From complexion

White be the brahmin
Vermillion be the kshatriya
Amber be the vaishya
Is not the case

Black be the shudra
Is not the distinction
Essence of life
Is the very same

Baheni says complexion
Does not make the brahmin
Scrutinise it thoroughly
In your mind

●✧✧●

7.

Now if we say
Caste makes the brahmin
That criterion seems
To be mindless

Keep aside everything
Ask the Vedas
What is left in the end
Be the answer

Rishi Shrungi was
Born to a deer
Rishi Gautam was
Born of kush* grass

Jambuk rishi was
Born of jamun tree
Valmiki's clan is found
In the anthill

Vyas was born
To a fisherwoman
Vishvamitra was born
To a kshatriya

Rishi Vasishtha was
Born to Urvashi
Agasti was born
Out of a mud pitcher

Narad is renowned
Known to everyone
A maidservant gave
Birth to him

Baheni says caste
Never makes the brahmin
Key to brahminness
Is very different

●~ঞৡ~●

*Desmostachya bipinnata

8.

Now if we say
The erudite be the brahmin
That too does not actually
Make any sense

Discerning rationale
Better be employed
The brahmin is truly
The enlightened one

Kshatriya, vaishya
Shudra, brahmin all

Erudition unforeseen
Exhibit all of them

Able to elucidate
Verse and matter
Knowledge of sciences
Poetics too

Muslims and others too
Exhibit erudition
Who can call them
The brahmins at all?

Baheni says thus
Examine the people
To determine who is
Genuinely the brahmin

9.

Now if we call those the brahmin
Who perform deeds designated
All the four varnas have
Deeds designated

How to call them the brahmin
For their deeds designated?
The key to brahminness
Is very different

All the varnas perform
Their deeds designated
That cannot qualify them
To be the brahmin

Baheni says the examination
Of deeds designated reveals
The brahminness lies beyond
Deeds designated

●❦❧●

10.

If we say duties designated
Determine the brahmin
It appears obviously
Unsubstantiated

The brahmin is disparate
Known by the knowledgeable
The enlightened ones
Recognize intuitively

Brahmin, kshatriya
Vaishya and shudras
Duties designated
Obligatory to all

Giving away food
Riches, cows and such

All the four varnas are
Obliged to

Baheni says duties designated
Do not make the brahmin
The criterion is different
For brahminness

●~꒰꒱~●

11.

Who is the brahmin
Will speak of it now
Wherein is stored
The gist of the Vedas

Upheld by the Vedas
As the epitome
That be the Guru for all
Paramount

No one else is greater
Than the brahmin
The Absolute is attained
In whose company

Whose words make
The salvation attainable
Whose one glimpse destroys
All the sins amassed

Supreme Being and the brahmin
Differ not even by an iota
Attain this very unification
In their company

Baheni says who knows
The key to brahminness
The wise try conscientiously
To find it out

● ‿୧ ୨‿ ●

12.

Though within the attributes[1]
Stays beyond their effects
Does not get ensnared ever
By the acts of the senses

Recognize among the masses
That be the only brahmin
Who knows no discrimination
Even in dreams

Devoid of the six drives[2]
Beyond the six modifications[3]
Unaffected by the multitudes
Of the vices

Baheni says upholder
Of the truth forever
Know that be the brahmin
Decisively

●๑๛●

1. Three attributes (त्रिगुण) - *Sattva* (सत्त्व goodness, constructive, harmonious), *raja* (रज passion, active, confused) and *tama* (तम darkness, destructive, chaotic) are the three attributes i.e. *triguna* which define each and every living being.

2. *Shadurmi* (षड्ऊर्मी) – *pipasa* (पिपासा thirst), *kshudha* (क्षुधा pangs of hunger, appetite), *shoka* (शोक sorrow, suffering), *moha* (मोह temptation, infatuation, delusion), *jara* (जरा old age), and *mrityu* (मृत्यू death)

3. *Shadbhav* (षड्भाव) - *Asti* (अस्ति existence), *Jayate* (जायते birth), *Vardhate* (वर्धते growth), *Viparinamate* (विपरिणमते change), *Apaksheeyate* (अपक्षीयते decay), *Vinashyate* (विनश्यते destruction)

13.

Absorption* in the Supreme Being
Without self-consciousness
Whose mind has attained
So exquisite

That one and only be truly
The brahmin as per the Vedas
All other expositions thereof
Are acts of heresy

Perceives the Supreme Being
Among all living beings

The very personification who is
Of equanimity

Baheni says like
The sky is everywhere
The brahmin commingles
With the world

●⚬⚘●

Nirvikalpa Samadhi (निर्विकल्प समाधी) - Complete mergence with the Supreme Being, in which there is no consciousness of the triad of the one who aspires to know (*dnyata* ध्याता), the object of the knowledge (*dneya* ज्ञेय) and the process of the knowledge (*dnyan* ज्ञान)

14.

Within and without
Perpetual indivisible
Who experiences the Unfathomable
Unadulterated

That alone be called
The brahmin, know this well
Whose ultimate goal be
The Supreme Being

For whom selflessness
Is all the chattels
Whose hands are ever ready
To help the needy

Baheni says lust
Anger all departed
Only therein resides
Brahminness

● ⚘ ●

15.

Abilities to subdue the senses
Attained all nine
Who is ever steeped
In contentment

Superior than the superior
Is the brahmin formidable
Who bestows salvation
Upon the degenerate

Cravings, attachment, hypocrisy
Vanity all departed
Who performs all his deeds
Without affectations

Baheni says whose
Desire extinguished
That be the brahmin
Devoted to the Supreme Being

● ⚘ ●

16.

Whose being is steeped ever
In the Supreme Being
That be the brahmin
One and only

On the authority of the Scriptures
I have stated all this
I have not indulged
In vague statements

Within the Supreme Being
Immersed all the senses
Therefore termed
As the brahmin

Baheni says the brahmin is that
Who inhabits the Supreme Being
The caste has no bearing there
Whatsoever

●❧❧●

भ्रतारे मारिले मोट बांधोनिया

My husband had beaten*
Hand & legs tied up
The calf could not bear
To see the sufferings

On the fourth day
The calf died
Vitthal performed
A miracle

Appeared in the form
Of a brahmin and told
Make your mind watchful
Henceforth

I kept my heart
Vigilant all the time
I wove up my mind
With Tukoba

On the seventh day
After the calf's departure
Tukaram appeared
In my dream

He consoled me
Gave the nectar to drink

He let the cow
Meet her calf

After the nectar
Gave me the mantra
Which people chant
Everywhere

He graced me
His hand on my head
He alone knows
The Form Supreme

The glory of his grace
Is but infinite
The calf could recite
Remaining half of the shloka

On the eighth day
Regained consciousness
With Tukaram's nectar
Fully satiated

Then I saw the cow
In front of me
Then I came to know
The calf died

Saying, this calf
Was given the nectar
She will not face
Death ever

That calf immortal
Resides with me
The sweetness of the nectar
The mind partakes

Baheni says thus
It transpired till that time
I will also narrate next
Expansively

● ৵৩ ●

*Some scholars have declared this abhang to be an interpolation, owing to its narrative repetitions. However, there are many more such abhang with narrative repetitions in Bahinabai's Gatha, which are not considered interpolations. A better way to explain the existence of such repetitive abhang is multiple attempts at writing autobiographies at different stages of life on Bahinabai's part.

Appendix III
Bilingual list of the first lines

The Autobiography of Sant Bahinabai

1.	Devgaon is the place	देवगाव माझे माहेर साजणी
2.	Devgaon is the place	देवगाव माझे माहेर साजणी (KT)
3.	Aauji Kulkarni	आऊजी कुलकर्णी लेखक
4.	There were celebrations	करिती उत्साह बारसा ब्राम्हण
5.	Other girls would play	लोकांचिया मुली खेळती बोळकी
6.	Brahmins would arrive	कन्यादान घडो हा अर्थ पाहोन
7.	My father belongs	मौनस गोत्र माझ्या पित्याचे वरिष्ठ
8.	My dear parents	मातापितयाने लग्न संपादिले
9.	Four years after	लग्न संपादोनी झाली वरुषे चारी
10.	Having seen Godavari	गंगा देखोनिया सिद्धेश्वर देव
11.	Asking for alms	मागोनी भिक्षेसी क्रमितसे वाट
12.	On Chaitra Pornima	चैत्र पौर्णिमेस गेलो महादेवा
13.	My husband asked us	भ्रतार विचारी सर्वांस विचार
14.	All settled down	रहेमतपुरी सर्व जाउनी राहिलो
15.	Went to Pandhari	चालले पंढरी महादेवाहूनी
16.	Hirambhat one there	हिरंभट एक ब्राम्हण वेदांती
17.	Husband would conduct rites	वैदिक व्यवहार स्वामी उदरार्थ
18.	Chanting Lord's name	नामाचा विटाळ आमुचिये घरी
19.	All the Vedas call out	वेद हाका देती पुराणे गर्जती
20.	A woman's body	स्त्रियेचे शरीर पराधीन देह
21.	What sins committed	काय पाप केले पूर्वील ये जन्मीं
22.	My being has undergone	सोसियेले क्लेश जीवे बहू फार
23.	This body is but destined	देहाचिया माथा सुखदुःख आले
24.	Strides of Fate	प्रारब्धाची गती न संडी सर्वथा
25.	My parents and brother are	मातापिता बंधू प्रपंचाचे सखे
26.	My brother, my companion	सखा सहोदर तूंचि एक हरी
27.	Origin of detachment	विरक्तीचे मूळ प्रपंचाचा त्याग
28.	Filled with penitence	अनुतापे तापले बहुत मानसी
29.	Like the deer fallen	हरण सापडे जैसे वाघुरेत
30.	On one occasion	कोण्ही एके वेळे अठराव्या वरुषांत
31.	With parents and brother	पिता माता बंधू समवेत बि-हाडी
32.	You may torture my body	गांजविसी देह भ्रताराचे हाते
33.	To his heart's content	आले मन ताव मारिले बळकट
34.	Wouldn't eat fodder	न खाती ते तृण न घेती जीवन

35.	Jayram Swami then	स्वस्थाना आपण चालले जयराम
36.	*Dwadashi* went by	द्वादशी क्रमोनी त्रयोदशी आत
37.	Soon the news	जयराम स्वामीस कळला वृत्तांत
38.	Opening my eyes	उघडोनिया नेत्र पाहे जव पुढे
39.	Fish without water	मच्छ जैसा जळावाचूनी तडफडी
40.	Who can incinerate	संचितासी दग्ध करी ऐसा कोण
41.	Cannot utter a word	न बोलवे शब्द अंतरीचा धावा
42.	Great lamentation	बहुत अंतरी शोक आरंभिला
43.	Attained contentment	झाले समाधान ब्राम्हणाच्या शब्दे
44.	Jayram eminent	जयराम समर्थ ज्ञानाचा सागर
45.	Jayram Swami	कृपा उपजली जयराम स्वामीसी
46.	A glance of grace	मजवरी दृष्टी कृपेची वोतली
47.	Such was amazement	नवल जनासी वाटले म्हणोनी
48.	My husband would say	भ्रतार म्हणतसे आम्ही की ब्राम्हण
49.	My husband had made	विचारिले मनी भ्रतारे आपण
50.	He'd say, O mind	म्हणे आता मना स्त्रियेची हे दशा
51.	What can be done	काय म्या अदृष्टा करावे आपण
52.	If husband goes away	भ्रतार गेलिया वैराग्य घेऊनी
53.	Upon husband's	भ्रतारे वैराग्य घेतलिया वरी
54.	Vitthal is of rocks	पाषाण विठ्ठल स्वप्नातील तुका
55.	My husband had	भ्रतारे निश्चय केला वनामाजी
56.	Then arrived an elderly	वृध्दसा ब्राम्हण येऊनी बोलत
57.	My husband regained	आरोग्य तत्काळ व्यथेचा हरास
58.	The mother of the calf	वत्साचिये माय कपिला सांगाते
59.	Today my life has become	आजि माझा जन्म सफल गे माये
60.	Noontime was nigh	माध्यान्ह जालीया पाहिजे ते अन्न
61.	Mambaji Gosavi/Was a	मंबाजी गोसावी त्या स्थळी नांदता
62.	Kirtan in the temple	देऊळात कथा सर्व काळ होत
63.	Mambaji Gosavi/Said	मंबाजी गोसावी भ्रतारासी म्हणे
64.	One day on the way	एके दिवशी वाटे देखील आपण
65.	Mahadaji Kulkarni/Told	महादाजी कुलकर्णी कोंडाजी
66.	My devotion is not	नव्हे करणीची आहाच
67.	Apaji Gosavi/Resided at Pune	आपाजी कुलकर्णी पुण्यात राहत
68.	Apaji Gosavi/Read the letter	आपाजी गोसावी वाचोनिया पत्र
69.	Mambaji's heart was	मंबाजी गोसावी द्वेष करी जीवे
70.	The cow from Kolhapur	कोल्हापुरी गाय होती ते सांगाते
71.	Rameshwar Bhatt	रामेश्वरभटे ऐकला वृत्तांत
72.	Mahadaji Kulkarni/Had	महादाजी कुलकर्णी तयाचिये घरी
73.	Sins amassed exhausted	तुटले संचित झाले शुद्ध चित्त

74.	The verandah of the temple	आनंदवोवरी होती तये ठायी
75.	Knew no meditation	नेणे जप तप नेणे अनुष्ठान
76.	Joy overwhelmed	आनंदे सद्गद जाहली इंद्रिये
77.	Describing that Bliss	ते सुख सांगता वाचे पडे मौन
78.	I felt I shouldn't get up	वाटे उठो नये जीव जाय तरी
79.	Farewell to Rukmini	रुक्मिणीची आम्ही केली बोळवण
80.	Receiving the letter	ऐकोनिया पत्र आलासी तातडी
81.	I have listened earnestly	ऐकियले तुझे वचन सादर
82.	Holy waters, pilgrimages	तीर्थ देव यात्रा वर्तता स्वधर्म
83.	Godavari, Bhagirathi	गोदा भागीरथी यमुना सरस्वती
84.	What holy waters can equal	आत्मज्ञाना ऐसे कोण तीर्थ दुजे
85.	At my final moments	अंतकाळ वेळ होईल निरभ्र
86.	Seventy two years	तेरावा तो जन्म देह वर्ते हाची
87.	Thirteen births today	तेरा जन्म तुज सांगितले आज
88.	At the time of death	मृत्यूचे प्रसंगी असावे सावध
89.	Facing the North	आसनी बैसोन उत्तराभिमुख
90.	With the blessings of the Saints	संतकृपा झाली

Sant Bahinabai's Translation of the Vajrasuchi Upanishad

1.	Among the four Varnas	चहू वर्णामाजी वरिष्ठ ब्राम्हण
2.	Who is to be called	ब्राम्हण कोणासी म्हणावे निश्चित
3.	Being is the brahmin	जीव हा ब्राम्हण म्हणावे इत्यर्थ
4.	Body is the brahmin	देहची ब्राम्हण म्हणो जरी आता
5.	Dotage, death, fear	जरा मृत्यू भय सर्वांसी समान
6.	Now if we determine	आता वर्ण हाची ब्राम्हण म्हणावा
7.	Now if we say/Caste makes	आता याती लागी म्हणावे ब्राम्हण
8.	Now if we say/The erudite	आता म्हणो जरी ब्राम्हण पंडिता
9.	Now if we call those the	आता म्हणो जरी कर्म ते ब्राम्हण
10.	If we say duties designated	आता धर्म यासी म्हणावे ब्राम्हण
11.	Who is the brahmin	ब्राम्हण तो एक सांगेन इत्यर्थ
12.	Though within the attributes	गुणांत असोनी गुणांसी नातळे
13.	Absorption in the Supreme	निर्विकल्प जया समाधी जोडली
14.	Within and without	अंतर्बाह्य एक अखंड अदृश्य
15.	Abilities to subdue the senses	शमदम सर्व साधिले नवगुण
16.	Whose being is steeped ever	ब्रह्मभाव देही सदासर्वकाळ

SOURCE TEXTS

The Umarkhane Text and the Kolharkar Text can be accessed on Sitaram Mhatre Foundation's Sant Bahinabai Gatha webpage: **https://www.sitarammhatre.foundation/sant-bahinabai-gatha**

All the Marathi abhang translated in this book also can be accessed
on the Foundation's website, here:
https://www.sitarammhatre.foundation/autobiography-of-sant-bahinabai

ABOUT THE AUTHOR

Chandrakant Kaluram Mhatre (MA, BEd, MPhil, PGDT, SET, NET) is a bilingual poet and a professional translator from Navi Mumbai, Maharashtra. His other books include: *One Hundred Poems of Chokha Mela, One Hundred Poems of Tukaram, Crumbs of Me* and *Nine: A Short Story Collection.* Currently, he is also leading a team of proof-readers working on Sitaram Mhatre Foundation's 'Bhakti Literature in Unicode' Project.
For more details, please visit:
www.sitarammhatre.foundation/shabdaagar